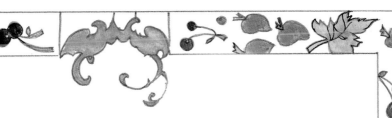

AMERICAN BIBLE SOCIETY

READ and LEARN

Family Faith Treasury

A Year of Inspirational Stories

Selected and Edited by Eva Moore

SCHOLASTIC INC.

New York   Toronto   London   Auckland   Sydney
Mexico City   New Delhi   Hong Kong   Buenos Aires

ISBN 0-439-87201-4

12 11 10 9 8 7 6 5 4 3 2 1   6 7 8 9 10 11/0

Color illustrations by José Miralles
Grayscale illustrations by González Vicente
Book design by Joan Moloney

Printed in Singapore
First printing, November 2006

Table of Contents

Introduction

Reading together with a child is one of the most satisfying experiences a person can have. It is a time to share enjoyment in the written word and to exchange thoughts and ideas that bring you closer to each other.

The *Read and Learn Family Faith Treasury* provides many opportunities for this kind of special sharing experience. You will find favorite stories and verses from the Bible, simple fables of Aesop with their wise messages, and engaging tales and poems relevant to the month in which they appear.

These selections exemplify values that we all want to instill in young people—honesty; humility; love; kindness; forgiveness; knowledge and industry; generosity; courage; respect for one's parents, country, fellow human beings, and all of God's creatures; reverence for and faith in God.

The *Read and Learn Family Faith Treasury* may be enjoyed on two levels: as a year-round collection that celebrates the spiritual joys and notable days particular to each month, and as a book of virtues. Biblical quotes that precede or follow most of the selections provide the key to a story's theme. In January, for example, the account of Jacob and Esau and the excerpt from *The Adventures of Pinocchio* show forgiveness; justice and kindness to one's fellow human beings are conveyed in the true story about Dr. Martin Luther King Jr., whose birthday we celebrate that month.

In exploring virtues, leaf through the volume to locate selections that apply. If your topic is love and kindness, you'll find stories in February ("Naomi and Ruth" and "The Lion and the Mouse"), May ("Johnny Appleseed and the Pioneers"), and October ("The Real Neighbor" and "Pleasing the Lord"). Stories about courage and faith in God include "Into the Promised Land" and "The Old Fox" in July, "Betsy and the Creepy House" in August, and "Saint George and the Dragon" in October.

Many stories encompass more than one virtue. For example, another illustration of forgiveness will be found in the Bible narration about the two sons (November), which also includes a message about giving thanks. "Sarah and the Kitten" (May) combines humility, kindness, and respect for animals. You may want to read this in conjunction with "Ladders to Heaven" (March), a legend about humility and the love of nature, and "The Birds' Gift" (April), a sweet tale that celebrates the bond between people and God's creatures. The stories about Dr. Martin Luther King Jr. (January), Abraham Lincoln (February), and George Washington (July) may be read in tandem as examples of American heroes whose lives were guided by the Bible and shaped by their faith in God.

Another option is, of course, to choose selections according to your heart's desire. But no matter how you approach the collection, you and your child will find treasures to enjoy over and over again at any time of the year.

— Eva Moore

January

Here we bring new water
from the well so clear,
For to worship God with,
this happy New Year.

from "A New Year Carol"

If you forgive others for the wrongs they do to you, your Father in heaven will forgive you.

— Matthew 6:14

From the Bible

Jacob and Esau

based on GENESIS 25:31-33

Jacob and Esau were the sons of Isaac and Rebekah. They were twins, but they did not look exactly alike.

Esau had been born first. When he grew up, he was big and brawny. His skin was tanned and he had hair on his hands, arms, and neck. He was a hunter and spent a lot of time away from home.

Jacob had fair, smooth skin. He was a quiet man who stayed home and farmed the land.

Their father, Isaac, was the leader of a people blessed by God. His father, Abraham, had been the first leader. Now Isaac was old and could hardly see.

By custom, he had to pass on God's blessing to his older son, Esau, so that he would become the new leader. But God had told Isaac's wife, Rebekah, that the younger son was the one who was meant to lead the people.

So Rebekah made Jacob dress in Esau's best clothes. Then she put hairy goatskins on Jacob's arms and hands to make them feel like Esau's. When Isaac called for Esau, Rebekah sent Jacob to Isaac's bedside instead.

Isaac knew the smell of Esau's clothes. He touched Jacob's hands and thought they were the hands of Esau. He gave Jacob his blessing and made him the next leader of the people.

When Esau found out, he was very angry. He said he would kill Jacob. So Rebekah sent Jacob away to live with her brother in a village far away.

The years passed. Jacob lived in his uncle's village. He had a large family of his own. He had herds of sheep, goats, cattle, donkeys, and camels.

One day, God came to Jacob and told him to return to the land of his father, Isaac.

Jacob's mother, Rebekah, had died. Jacob had not seen his father in twenty years. He wanted to go back to his old home. But he was afraid to meet his brother. What if Esau was still angry with him?

Jacob had an idea. He asked his servants to take some animals to Esau as a gift. There were 220 goats and 220 sheep; there were 30 mother camels and their young; there were 50 cattle and 30 donkeys.

After the animals arrived, Jacob went to meet Esau. When Esau saw Jacob, he ran to him and put his arms around him. The brothers wept tears of joy.

"Why did you send all these animals?" Esau asked. "I already have plenty."

Each had gone his own way, just as God had meant them to. Now God had brought them together again.

See that justice is done and be kind and merciful to one another!

— Zechariah 7:8-9

On the third Monday of every January, the United States honors an American hero named Martin Luther King Jr. Dr. King, a Baptist minister, was born on January 15, 1929, and died in 1968. Why do we honor this minister? Here is a true story that tells you.

Singing for Dr. King

by Angela Shelf Medearis

In 1965, Sheyann Webb was in the third grade in Selma, Alabama. She was smaller than most third-graders, including her best friend, Rachel West.

Rachel was nine. She lived with her family in the apartment next door to Sheyann's.

Sheyann's family went to church services at Brown Chapel on Sunday mornings. It was just a block away from the Webbs' apartment building.

One Sunday in January 1965, Sheyann listened as a special guest preacher spoke. He was Dr. Martin Luther King Jr. He preached about working together so that African Americans could have the freedom to vote.

Dr. King said that he wanted every American, no matter what color, to enjoy the same rights under the law. These rights are called civil rights. Dr. King believed that voting was one way to change laws in the South that were unfair to black people.

Sheyann listened as Dr. King's voice thundered through the chapel. His words were powerful and strong. She knew he was right about the way African Americans were treated in Selma. Her oldest sister, Vivian, had marched for civil rights. She had been arrested just for marching. Sheyann wanted to work for civil rights, just like Vivian.

In Selma, it was easy for white people to register to vote. African Americans would sometimes have to stand in line all day when they went to register.

Sheyann knew that this was not fair.

Day after day, hundreds of African Americans lined up to register. Day after day, only a few would be allowed to sign up. But the others did not give up. They kept coming back.

For the first time, Sheyann saw many African Americans working together for their rights.

One day, when Sheyann was on her way to school, she saw a crowd at Brown Chapel. What was going on? Sheyann went inside to see. She was the only child there.

The people in the church were planning more marches for voting rights. Someone asked Sheyann to come to the next meeting and lead the singing. He told Sheyann that they wanted her to sing freedom songs.

Freedom songs are old church songs with some new words added about freedom. Singing freedom songs gave the marchers courage as they walked along. Freedom songs let everyone who was listening know the purpose of the march.

Sheyann was a little afraid. She had never sung before a crowd of people. She was just a little girl. She couldn't register to vote, but she could sing for Dr. King. Singing was something Sheyann could do to help the Civil Rights Movement. She agreed to be a song leader.

Sheyann told Rachel about singing for Dr. King. Rachel wanted to go to the meetings and help Dr. King, too.

That night, Sheyann and Rachel put on their best dresses. They put ribbons in their hair. Then they went to Brown Chapel.

Dr. King would be arriving the next morning, January 19, 1965. He would lead a march for civil rights.

More than 800 people filled the church that night. Everyone talked about working peacefully for their civil rights. . . .

Then it was Sheyann's turn to sing.

Sheyann got up and looked at all the people. She remembered what Dr. King had said about being brave. She was afraid, but she started to sing. Then Rachel got up to sing with her. . . . Sheyann and Rachel sang freedom songs together. Everyone joined in!

Sheyann led the songs during more meetings at Brown Chapel. She led songs during protest marches, too. Then protesters sang with Sheyann as they marched along the streets and bridges of Selma. They sang when people called them names. They sang when they were put in jail. The words of the freedom songs made them all feel braver.

At first, Sheyann's mother and father did not want her to march. They were afraid she might get hurt or be put in jail. Her parents were afraid that if they marched, they might lose their jobs.

Sheyann told them that she wanted her family to help Dr. King.

One day, Sheyann's parents asked her what she wanted for her ninth birthday. She said that all she wanted was for them to join the marches and register to vote.

The next morning, her parents said they had an early birthday present for her. They were going to march! Sheyann hugged them both.

Later that day, along with many other marchers, Sheyann's parents walked to the courthouse to try to register to vote. They sang freedom songs all the way. They sang about marching for civil rights. They sang about getting the right to vote. They sang about being free.

> *I'll keep walking.*
> *I'll keep talking.*
> *I'll keep marching*
> *Up to freedom land!*

Millions of Americans saw the marches on television. They read about them in the newspapers. People came from all over to join the marchers in Selma. . . .

President Lyndon Baines Johnson got thousands of calls and

letters. People were upset about the cruel way the marchers were being treated. They asked him to change the laws. They wanted every American to be treated fairly and equally.

Dr. King met with President Johnson on March 5, 1965. . . . Dr. King asked him to pass the Voting Rights Act. This new law said that every American of every race had the right to vote.

On August 6, 1965, President Johnson signed the Voting Rights Act into law.

Dr. King dreamed of a day when every American would be treated equally. Today, Americans are still working together to make that dream come true. . . .

> Jesus said, ". . . forgive the ones who say they are sorry. Even if one of them mistreats you seven times in one day and says, 'I am sorry,' you should still forgive that person."
>
> — Luke 17:3-4

Pinocchio's Promise

from *The Adventures of Pinocchio* by C. Collodi

Once upon a time there was a piece of wood. Out of that piece of wood the carpenter Geppetto carves a boy puppet (or marionette), with a long nose and a laughing mouth. To Geppetto's surprise and delight, the puppet comes to life. He names the puppet Pinocchio and cares for him as if he were a real boy. But Pinocchio cannot behave. Very soon he runs away in search of adventure.

And adventure is what he gets — sometimes very frightening and unpleasant adventure. Once, when he was very sick, a kind, blue-haired Fairy helped save his life, but many others he met got him into a lot of trouble.

Now Pinocchio is trying to get back to Geppetto, his father, but the way is not easy. After landing on an island, he finds himself in a place called the Land of the Busy Bees. He has not had anything to eat or drink for a long time. He tries to beg for food but the people just pass him by, telling him he should work to earn his own bread.

Finally, a small woman went by. She was carrying two water jugs.

"Good woman, will you allow me to have a drink from one of your jugs?" asked Pinocchio, who was burning up with thirst.

"With pleasure, my boy!" she answered, setting the two jugs on the ground before him.

When Pinocchio had had his fill, he said, grumbling as he wiped his mouth, "My thirst is gone. If I could only as easily get rid of my hunger!"

On hearing these words, the good woman immediately said, "If you will carry one of these jugs to my house, I'll give you a slice of bread."

Pinocchio looked at the jug and said neither yes nor no.

"And with the bread, I'll give you a nice dish of cauliflower with white sauce on it."

Pinocchio gave the jug another look and said neither yes nor no.

"And after the cauliflower, some cake and jam."

At this, Pinocchio could no longer resist. "Very well, I'll take the jug home for you."

When they arrived, the woman made Pinocchio sit down at a small table and placed before him the bread, the cauliflower, and the cake. Pinocchio did not just eat. He devoured. His stomach seemed a bottomless pit.

His hunger finally satisfied, he raised his head to thank the kind woman. But he had not looked at her long when he gave a cry of surprise and sat there with his eyes wide open, his fork in the air, and his mouth filled with bread and cauliflower.

"Why such surprise?" asked the good woman, laughing.

"Because," answered Pinocchio, stammering and stuttering, "because you look like — you remind me of — yes, yes, the same voice, the same eyes, the same hair — yes, yes, yes, you also have the same blue hair she had! Oh, my little Fairy! Tell me that it is you! If only you knew! I have cried so much, I have suffered so!"

If Pinocchio cried like this much longer, the woman thought he would melt away, so she finally admitted that she was the little Fairy with the blue hair.

"You rascal of a marionette! How did you know it was I?" she asked, laughing.

"My love for you told me who you were."

"Do you remember?" she said. "You left me when I was a little girl and now you find me a grown woman. I am so old, I could almost be your mother!"

"I am very glad of that, for then I can call you mother instead of sister," said Pinocchio. "For a long time I have wanted a mother, just like other boys. But how did you grow so quickly?"

"That's a secret!"

"Tell it to me. I also want to grow a little. Look at me! I have never grown higher than a penny's worth of cheese."

"But you can't grow," answered the Fairy.

"Why not?"

"Because marionettes never grow. They are born marionettes, they live as marionettes, and they die as marionettes."

"Oh, I'm tired of always being a marionette!" cried Pinocchio. "It's about time for me to grow into a man as everyone else does."

"And you will, if you deserve it."

"Really? What can I do to deserve it?"

"It's a very simple matter. Try to act like a well-behaved child."

"Don't you think I do?"

"Far from it!" the Fairy said. "Good boys are obedient, and you, on the contrary —"

"And I never obey," Pinocchio said.

"Good boys love to study and work, and you —"

"And I, on the contrary, am a lazy fellow."

"Good boys always tell the truth."

"And I always tell lies," Pinocchio admitted.

"Good boys go gladly to school."

"And I get sick if I go to school. From now on I'll be different."

"Do you promise?" asked the Fairy.

"I promise. I want to become a good boy and be a comfort to my father. Where is my poor father now?"

"I don't know."

"Will I ever be lucky enough to find him?" Pinocchio asked.

"I think so," the Fairy said. "Indeed, I am sure of it."

At this answer, Pinocchio's happiness was very great. He looked into the Fairy's eyes.

"Tell me, Mother. It isn't true you are dead, is it?"

"It doesn't seem so," answered the Fairy, smiling.

"If only you knew how I suffered and how I wept when I thought you were dead."

"I know it, and because of that I have forgiven you. The depth of your sorrow made me see that you have a kind heart. There is always hope for boys with hearts such as yours, though they may often be very mischievous. This is the reason I have come so far to look for you. From now on, I'll be your own little mother."

Pinocchio began to jump with joy.

The Fairy went on. "You will obey me always and do as I wish?"

"Gladly, very gladly, more than gladly," Pinocchio cried.

"Beginning tomorrow," said the Fairy, "you'll go to school every day."

Pinocchio's face fell a little.

"Then you will choose the trade you like best."

Pinocchio became more serious.

"What are you mumbling to yourself?" asked the Fairy.

"I was just saying," whined the marionette in a whisper, "that it seems too late for me to go to school now."

"No, indeed. Remember, it is never too late to learn."

"But I don't want a trade or a profession," Pinocchio insisted.

"Why?" the Fairy asked.

"Because work makes me tired!"

"My dear boy," said the Fairy, "people who speak as you do usually end their days in a prison or in a hospital. A man, remember, whether rich or poor, should do something in this world. No one can find happiness without work. Woe to the lazy fellow! Laziness is a serious illness and one must cure it immediately; yes, even from early childhood. If not, it will kill you in the end."

These words touched Pinocchio's heart. He lifted his eyes to his Fairy and said seriously, "I'll work. I'll study. I'll do all you tell me, and I want to become a boy, no matter how hard it is. You promise that, don't you?"

The Fairy smiled. "Yes," she said, "I promise. And now it is up to you."

February

Your heart will always be
where your treasure is.

— *Matthew 6:21*

My dear friends, we must love each other. Love comes from God. . . .

No one has ever seen God. But if we love each other, God lives in us, and his love is truly in our hearts.

— 1 John 4:7, 12

From the Bible

Naomi and Ruth

based on RUTH 1-4

Naomi lived in the country of Moab, but she had not been born there. She came from the town of Bethlehem, in the land of Judah, which was part of Israel. Naomi and her husband and their two sons had moved across the Jordan River to Moab when their land in Judah dried up and they could no longer grow crops to support themselves.

Not many Israelites lived in Moab because it was considered a country of enemies. At first, Naomi was sad in her new home.

After a while, Naomi's husband died. When her two sons grew up, both of them married women from Moab. One son married a woman named Orpah. The other married a woman named Ruth.

Then Naomi's sons died, too. Naomi and her sons' wives, Ruth and Orpah, were alone.

Naomi felt lonely. She wanted to go back to Bethlehem to be with her own people again.

One day, Naomi packed up her few clothes and set out on the road to Bethlehem. Orpah and Ruth went with her. They had not gone far when Naomi stopped. She told her daughters-in-law to go back. She knew it would be easier for them to find new husbands in their own land than as strangers in Bethlehem. She wanted them to be happy.

Orpah turned around and headed back to Moab. But Ruth loved Naomi as if she were her own mother. She said, "Please don't tell me to leave you and return home! I will go where you go, and I will live where you live; your people will be my people, your God will be my God."

And so Ruth went to Bethlehem with her mother-in-law. They were poor. Ruth picked up bits of grain from a farmer's field to make their bread.

The farmer, Boaz, noticed Ruth. He thought she was brave to leave her own people and kind to look after her mother-in-law. He grew to love her, even though she was not an Israelite.

Ruth and Boaz got married. They had a baby boy, and they named him Obed. Naomi was happy again.

Ruth's son, Obed, also had a son, Jesse. Jesse was the father of one of the greatest kings of Israel, David.

February 14 is Valentine's Day. It's a day to tell your family and friends that you love them by making and sending cards.

Sometimes you can be surprised when you open a valentine and find a new friend.

There's Someone I Know

There's someone I know
whom I simply can't stand,
I wish he would bury
his head in the sand,
or move to the moon
or to deep outer space,
whenever I see him
I make a weird face.

Today during recess
outside in the yard,
he suddenly gave me
a valentine card.
I wish that he hadn't,
it made me upset,
it was the prettiest one
I could possibly get.

— *Jack Prelutsky*

The Lion and the Mouse

from *Aesop's Fables*

Once when a lion was asleep, a little mouse began to run up and down his back. This made the lion wake up. With one swoop of his mighty paw, the lion pounced on the mouse and held her fast so she couldn't escape. Then he opened his mouth and was about to swallow the poor little creature.

The mouse spoke up. "O King," she said, "please forgive me for waking you. If you do, I will never forget it. And who knows? Maybe someday I will be able to do you a favor, too."

The lion thought this idea was so funny that he began to laugh and laugh. He lifted up his paw and let the mouse go.

Some time later, the lion found himself caught in a trap. The hunters wanted to take him to a zoo. They tied him to a tree while they went to get a wagon to carry him.

Just then, the little mouse happened to pass by. She took one look at the ropes and knew the lion was in trouble. So she went up to him and began to chew the ropes. Soon the lion was free.

"See," said the little mouse, "I was right!"

Little friends may prove great friends.

Abraham Lincoln was born on February 12, 1809, in a log cabin in Kentucky. His family was poor, but Abe and his older sister Sally were lucky to have a hardworking father and a stepmother who gave them a good home.

When Abe was fourteen, he sometimes did chores for his neighbors, Josiah and Elizabeth Crawford. Sally did housework for them. One day, Josiah Crawford let Abe borrow a book about George Washington. There was nothing Abe liked to do more than read. Reading opened up his life, and it also gave him all kinds of ideas.

Abe Speaks Out

from *Abe Lincoln Gets His Chance*

by Frances Cavannah

Abe sat up late, holding his book close to the flickering flames in the fireplace. As the rain drummed on the roof, his thoughts were far away. He was with General Washington in a small boat crossing the Delaware River on a cold Christmas night many years before. . . .

"Isn't it getting too dark for you to see?" Sarah called sleepily.

"Yes, Mamma."

Carefully, Abe placed the precious little volume between two logs in the wall of the cabin. This was his bookcase. As he climbed into the loft he wondered if the book told about the time George Washington became President. He would have to wait until morning to find out.

He was up early. But his face grew pale when he reached for the book. During the night the rain had leaked in through a crack in the logs. Its pages were wet and stuck together. . . . Sally was starting down the path toward the Crawford cabin when Abe called after her.

"Wait! I'm coming with you."

He thrust the book inside his buckskin shirt. Sally tried to comfort him, but Abe kept wondering what Mr. Crawford was going to say. He was a little scared of Josiah. Some of the boys called him Old Bluenose because of the large purple vein on the side of his nose. It made him look rather cross. He probably would want Abe to pay for the book, and Abe had no money.

He opened the Crawford gate and marched up to the kitchen door. Josiah, his wife, Elizabeth, and Sammy, their little boy, were having breakfast. When Abe explained what had happened, Mrs. Crawford patted his shoulder. He liked her. She was always nice to him, but he knew that her husband was the one who would decide about the book. Josiah took it in his big hands and looked at the stained pages.

"Well, Abe," he said slowly, "I won't be hard on you. If you want to pull fodder three days for me, that ought to pay for the book."

"Starting right now?"

"Yep, starting right now." Josiah was actually smiling. "Then you can have the book to keep."

Abe caught his breath. Three days' work and then he could keep the book! He could read about George Washington anytime he wanted.

Never had he worked harder or faster than he did that morning. When the noon dinner bell rang, he seemed to be walking on air as he followed Josiah into the cabin. His sister Sally was putting dinner on the table. Abe slipped up behind her and pulled one of her pigtails. Taken by surprise, she jumped and dropped a pitcher of cream. The pitcher did not break, but the cream spilled and spread over the kitchen floor.

"Abe Lincoln! Look what you made me do!" cried Sally. "I just washed that floor. And look at that good cream going to waste."

"'Tain't going to waste." Abe pointed to Elizabeth Crawford's cat, which was lapping up the delicious yellow stream. Then he began to sing: "Cat's in the cream jar, shoo, shoo, shoo!"

"Stop trying to show off!" said Sally.

She was angry, but Sammy, Elizabeth's little boy, shouted with delight. That was all the encouragement Abe needed. The fact that he could not carry a tune did not seem to bother him.

"Cat's in the cream jar, shoo, shoo, shoo!
Cat's in the cream jar, shoo, shoo, shoo!
Skip to my Lou, my darling."

Sally was down on her hands and knees, wiping up the cream. "Stop singing that silly song and help me."

Instead, Abe danced a jig. He leaned down and pulled her other pigtail.

"Sally's in the cream jar, shoo, shoo, shoo."

"That's enough, Abe," said Elizabeth Crawford.

"Skip to my Lou, my darling." He whirled around on his bare feet and made a sweeping bow. Sally was close to tears.

"Abe, I told you to stop," said Elizabeth Crawford. "You ought to be ashamed, teasing your sister. If you keep on acting that way, what do you think is going to become of you?"

"Me?" Abe drew himself up. "What's going to become of me? I'm going to be President."

Elizabeth looked at him, a lanky barefoot boy with trousers too short. His shirt was in rags. His black hair was tousled. She sank into a chair, shaking with laughter. "A pretty President you'd make, now, wouldn't you?"

She had no sooner spoken then she wanted to take back the words. All the joy went out of his face. Sally was too angry to notice.

"Maybe you're going to be President," she said. "But first you'd better learn to behave."

"I — I was just funning, Sally."

Something in his voice made Sally look up. She saw the hurt expression in his eyes. "I know you were," she said hastily. "I'm not mad anymore."

Abe ate his dinner in silence. He did not seem to be the same boy who had been cutting up only a few minutes before. Elizabeth kept telling herself that she should not have laughed at him. He did try to show off sometimes. But he was a good boy. . . . When he pushed back his stool, she followed him out into the yard.

"About your being President," she said. "I wasn't aiming to make fun of you. I just meant that you — with all your tricks and jokes —"

"I reckon I know what you meant," said Abe quietly. "All the same, Mrs. Crawford, I don't always mean to delve and grub and the like."

There was a look of determination on his face that she had not seen before. "I think a heap of you," she went on, "and I don't want to see you disappointed. It's a fine thing to be ambitious. But don't let reading about George Washington give you notions that can't come to anything."

Abe threw back his shoulders. "I aim to study and get ready and then the chance will come."

He lifted his battered straw hat and started down the path toward the field. He walked with dignity. Elizabeth had not realized that he was so tall.

"I declare," she said, "he really means it!"

Sammy had come up and heard her. "Means what, Mamma?" he asked.

Elizabeth took his hand. "Didn't you know, Sammy? Abe is fixing to be President some day."

Thirty-seven years later, in 1860, Abraham Lincoln became the sixteenth President of the United States.

One of Abe's favorite books when he was a boy was the Bible. Another was his stepmother's copy of *Aesop's Fables*. He read the stories again and again. You will find some of these stories in this book. The one below must have made an impression on Lincoln: when Abe grew up, people called him "Honest Abe."

The Boy Who Cried Wolf

from *Aesop's Fables*

There was once a young shepherd boy who watched over his sheep at the foot of a mountain near a dark forest. He found it rather dull and boring with only the sheep for company.

One day he came up with a plan to add some excitement to his life. He ran down to the village, calling out, "Wolf! Wolf!" The villagers thought that a wolf was after his sheep and came out to help. They followed the boy back to the foot of the mountain. Everything looked fine. None of the sheep were hurt.

"I *thought* I saw a wolf," the boy lied. Some of the villagers stayed just to make sure the sheep were safe.

The boy had such a good time that, a few days later, he tried the same trick. Again, the villagers came out to help him.

A few days afterward, a wolf actually did come out from the forest and start to stalk the sheep. "Wolf! Wolf!" the boy called out, louder than before. But this time the villagers thought that the boy was just playing games again, and nobody came to help.

So the wolf had a good meal off the boy's sheep. The boy went crying into the village: "Why didn't you help me?"

The wisest man in the village said:

"A liar will not be believed, even when he speaks the truth."

March

Flowers cover the earth,
it's time to sing.

— *Song of Songs 2:12*

God Is Like This

I cannot see the wind at all
Or hold it in my hand,
And yet I know there is a wind
Because it swirls the sand.
I know there is a wondrous wind
Because I glimpse its power
Whenever it bends low a tree
Or sways the smallest flower.

And God is very much like this,
Invisible as air.
I cannot touch or see Him, yet
I know that He is there
Because I glimpse His wondrous works
And goodness everywhere.

— *Rowena Bennett*

from *The Day Is Dancing and Other Poems*

The Story of Moses

based on EXODUS 2-32

The Hebrew people had lived in Egypt for hundreds of years. They had come from the land of Canaan. At first there were only a few families. But over the years they grew in number until there were too many to count.

Some of Egypt's rulers were worried that the Hebrews would someday take over the land. So they took away their rights and put them to work as slaves.

One of the Hebrews was named Moses. As a baby he had been adopted by the daughter of Pharaoh, the king, but when he grew up, he saw how cruelly the Egyptians treated the Hebrews. He left Egypt and lived as a shepherd.

One day, Moses was up in the mountains, tending his sheep. He came to a bush. The bush was on fire, but the fire was not burning the bush.

Moses came closer to get a better look. A voice came out of the fire! It was God speaking to him. God told him that He had seen the suffering of the Hebrew people in Egypt. He had chosen Moses to be the one to set them free and lead them to a special land that God had promised them long, long ago.

God told Moses to see Pharaoh and tell him to let the Hebrews go. Moses was a strong man, but he didn't think he was brave enough to face Pharaoh alone.

God said that Moses should take his brother Aaron with him. Aaron was a good speaker and would make Pharaoh listen.

Moses told his people that God was going to set them free. Then he and Aaron went to see Pharaoh.

"Our God has a message for you," Aaron said in his strong voice. "You must free our people and let us go out from Egypt."

Pharaoh laughed. "I'm not afraid of this Hebrew God. Why should I listen to you?"

Because the king would not listen to Moses and Aaron, God caused terrible things to happen in Egypt. First, He turned the water in the river to blood. He caused frogs, gnats, flies, and locusts to devastate the land. He sent diseases and darkness all over the land. He caused nine of these terrible plagues to afflict the people of Egypt, but Pharaoh would not let the Hebrews go.

Finally, Moses was sent to Pharaoh with a new message. "God says this to you: Every firstborn son in Egypt will die tonight. There will be great crying and wailing. Only the Hebrew sons will be spared." Moses told the Hebrews to mark their houses with lamb's blood so that they would be passed over when the plague came.

And so it happened. A great plague swept over the land. All the firstborn sons of Egypt died, including the son of Pharaoh.

At last the king was broken. "Go!" he said.

The Hebrews left in a hurry. They took pans of bread dough, for they did not have time to add the yeast and bake the bread.

Moses led the people across the desert to the Red Sea. Just as they got near the sea, they saw clouds of sand behind them. Pharaoh's army was coming! The king had changed his mind. He didn't want to lose the Hebrew slaves, so he sent his army to bring them back.

What could the people do? In back of them was the army, and in front of them, the sea. God came again to Moses. He said, "Lift up your staff, and stretch your hand over the sea."

Moses did as he was told. And lo! the waters of the sea divided. Between the two walls of water was dry ground so that the Hebrews could cross.

All the Hebrews got safely to the other side. Then Moses lifted his staff again, and the waters of the Red Sea flowed back together.

The sea covered the chariots and the horsemen who were chasing the Hebrews. Pharaoh's army was washed away.

The Hebrews sang and danced and praised God. They were free!

෨

God's Commandments

based on EXODUS 20:2-17

Three days after the people of Israel had escaped from Egypt, God called Moses once again. Moses went up to the top of a tall mountain. There God gave him the laws that He wanted the people to follow. The first ten laws were the most important. These Ten Commandments show God's people how to live with one another and how to honor God.

I am the Lord your God, the one who brought you out of Egypt where you were slaves. Do not worship any god except me.

Do not make idols that look like anything in the sky or on earth or in the ocean under the earth; don't bow down and worship idols.

Do not misuse my name.

Remember that the Sabbath Day belongs to me.

Respect your father and your mother.

Do not murder.

Be faithful in marriage.

Do not steal.

Do not tell lies about others.

Do not want anything that belongs to someone else.

Don't be jealous or proud, but be humble and consider others more important than yourselves.

— Philippians 2:3

A legend is a story that is based on something or someone from the real world. The stories about Johnny Appleseed (May) and St. George (October) are both legends. These men really lived, and we know that parts of the stories about them are true. But some parts were probably made up and passed along from one generation to the next. These men were so beloved that people were always adding to their good deeds.

This story about the lily of the valley is also a legend. No one can prove it really happened this way, but we know the flower comes up early every spring in soil that is damp and shaded, and that it is so hardy that it grows "like a weed."

Ladders to Heaven
—a Legend

adapted from the story by Julia Horatia Ewing

There was a certain valley in which the grass was very green, for it was watered by a stream that never dried up. Once upon a time, some holy men left their homes and built a monastery in the valley. They lived as brothers in their own private world.

The world outside in those days was very rough, and there was much warfare, but the little world in the Green Valley was quiet and peaceful. It was just the right place for a peaceful and quiet man like

Brother Benedict. Benedict planted a garden in the Green Valley. He grew herbs for healing, and plants that were good to eat, and flowers that took the breath away.

Each year, Brother Benedict added new plants and flowers to his garden. The garden became famous. Even people outside the Green Valley heard about it and wanted to see it.

Benedict kept a list of everything he planted. The list grew longer every spring and every autumn, and the garden became filled with rare and unusual things. Benedict looked at his garden and was filled with pride.

One day, a rich man from the outside world came to the Green Valley. This man also loved to grow things. When he told Brother Benedict about his garden, Benedict grew jealous. The man had a much larger garden with many more kinds of plants and flowers.

Later, Benedict felt greatly disturbed by the way he was feeling. He had always believed it was wrong to be jealous. And now he was having these feelings himself. *Maybe I should not be taking so much pride in my garden,* he thought. The next day he went to see the wise old man who lived by himself in a cave nearby. He asked the man what he should do.

"My son," said the old man, "if you take pride in work that is done for others, do not worry. He who lives for God and for his neighbors has a pure soul. For those who work in such a spirit, grace shall build ladders unto Heaven."

Benedict bowed his head and left the old man. When he got back home, he found a messenger who had come by horseback. The messenger had ridden many days to bring a package to Brother Benedict. Benedict unwrapped the package and found a bundle of roots with a note:

These roots, which are common with us, are not known in your land. It is a lily, as white and as sweet-smelling as the Easter lily, but much smaller. Beautiful as it is, it is hardy, and if planted in a damp spot and left alone to grow, it will spread like a weed. It has a rare and delicate perfume and white bells on a stalk, one above the other, as the angels stood in Jacob's dream. And so our children call the flower Ladders to Heaven.

Benedict's first thought was, *Ha! That rich man doesn't have a plant like this lily! It will be my very own.* But his second thought was, *God rid my soul of such pride! These flowers shall be for the common children, not for me.*

And so Benedict planted the roots in a little grove of trees where the earth was kept damp by the waters of the stream that never dried up. "The blessing of our Maker rest on these flowers," he prayed. "May they give joy to others when I am gone." Then he went back to his house. And he did not add the new plant to his list, for he had no such lily in his garden.

Many years passed. The outside world came to the Green Valley. All the houses fell to ruin and even Brother Benedict's garden was destroyed. But no one touched the lilies of the valley in the grove, for they were so common that they were looked upon as weeds.

And though people had forgotten all about the brothers who had lived there, the old tales were handed down. When children played with the lilies, they counted the flowers to see who had the most "angels." "My ladder has twelve white angels," a child would say, "and yours has only eight." Sometimes they called them Brother Benedict's flowers, adding, "but their real name is Ladders to Heaven."

Jacob's Ladder

based on GENESIS 27-28

Jacob was the son of Isaac, and the twin brother of Esau. When the twins were born, their mother, Rebekah, dreamed that God told her that Jacob would rule over Esau.

Now it was time for Isaac to bless the son who would lead God's people after he was gone. Since Esau was the firstborn, Isaac wanted him to be the new leader.

Rebekah knew this was not God's plan. So she dressed Jacob to look like Esau and sent him into Isaac's tent. It was dark in the tent and Isaac was nearly blind. He couldn't tell that he was blessing Jacob, not Esau.

When Esau found out, he was very angry. He said he would kill Jacob. So Rebekah sent Jacob away.

Jacob ran off into the desert. He walked all day. When the sun went down, he stopped to sleep.

There was a pile of stones nearby. Jacob took one of the stones and used it as a pillow.

That night, Jacob had a dream. He saw a great stairway, like a ladder, that went all the way up to Heaven. He saw angels climbing up and down the stairway. And there above them, he saw God.

God spoke to Jacob. "I will give you and all who come after you the land on which you are lying. I am with you always. I will watch over you no matter where you go, and one day, I will bring you back to this land."

Jacob woke up and remembered his dream. *How great is this place*, he thought. *This is the gate of Heaven*. He named the place Bethel, which means "the house of God."

You may also want to read the Bible story "Jacob and Esau" on page 3.

The Hares and the Frogs

from *Aesop's Fables*

The hares were always being chased by other animals. They didn't know where to go. As soon as they saw a single animal near them, off they would run. They were getting tired of all this running away.

One day, the hares saw a bunch of wild horses racing across the fields. As usual, the hares ran, some this way, some that. Some of them headed toward a lake. They thought it would be better to jump into the lake and drown rather than go on living in fear.

But when they reached the lake, a bunch of frogs sitting on the banks jumped into the water to get away from the hares.

The hares stopped. One of them said, "I guess things are not as bad as they seem."

There is always someone worse off than yourself.

April

Easter lilies! Can you hear
What they whisper, low and clear?...
Hark, their soft and heavenly chime!
Christ is risen for all time!

— *from "On Easter Day" by Celia Thaxter*

The Sunday before Easter is called Palm Sunday. Everyone who goes to church that day is given a palm branch. This story tells you why.

From the Bible

Jesus Comes to Jerusalem

based on LUKE 19:28-38

Jesus had decided to go to Jerusalem. When he and his disciples were near the city, he asked two of them to get a donkey for him. He said, "Go into the next village, where you will find a donkey that has never been ridden. Untie the donkey and bring it here. If anyone asks why you are doing that, just say, 'The Lord needs it.'"

The disciples went to the village and found the donkey. While they were untying it, its owners asked, "Why are you doing that?"

They answered, "The Lord needs it."

Then they led the donkey to Jesus. They put some of their clothes on its back and helped Jesus get on.

As Jesus came riding into Jerusalem, the people ran to greet him. They threw pieces of clothing and palm branches down onto the road in front of Jesus. This was the way they welcomed important people to the city.

The crowd cheered happily as Jesus rode past them:

"Blessed is the king who comes in the name of the Lord!
Peace in heaven and glory to God."

Jesus then said, "I am the one who raises the dead to life! Everyone who has faith in me will live, even if they die. And everyone who lives because of faith in me will never really die."

—John 11:25-26

The Good Shepherd

Psalm 23

You, Lord, are my shepherd.
I will never be in need.
You let me rest in fields
of green grass.
You lead me to streams of peaceful water,
and you refresh my life.

You are true to your name, and you lead me
along the right paths.
I may walk through valleys as dark as death,
but I won't be afraid.
You are with me, and your shepherd's rod
makes me feel safe.

You treat me to a feast,
while my enemies watch.
You honor me as your guest, and you fill my cup
until it overflows.

Your kindness and love will always be with me
each day of my life,
and I will live forever in your house, Lord.

Did you know that the Easter Bunny is not the only animal that decorates and delivers Easter eggs? This story comes from a country called Ukraine.

The Birds' Gift

A Ukrainian Easter Story

retold by Eric A. Kimmel

Grandfather Frost had come in the night, painting the windows with intricate patterns that looked like frozen flowers. Katrusya scratched the frost from the nearest pane. Snow covered the village as far as she could see. Suddenly, she jumped. An eye stared back at her from the other side of the windowpane. Grandfather! How he loved to play tricks! Icicles hung from the ends of his long mustache. As he spoke, the white clouds of his breath mingled with smoke from his pipe.

"Come outside before the others wake up. We have a world of snow all to ourselves."

Katrusya dressed quickly. She buttoned up her coat and covered her head with a *hustka*, a colorful scarf that the women of the village tied over their ears. She pulled a pair of thick felt boots over her woolen socks and hurried out the door.

"I knew winter would be early this year. I felt it in my bones. The grain is hardly in the barn. Sunflowers are still standing in the garden, and here comes the snow," Grandfather said.

The snow nearly reached the top of Katrusya's boots as she and her grandfather walked through the silent village, all the way to the forest. Grandfather stopped beneath a birch tree to shake snow from his hat. Katrusya stuck out her tongue to catch the flakes falling from the sky.

Suddenly, she stopped. "What's that?" Katrusya pointed to the foot of the tree. A fleck of gold shone like a buried coin through the snow.

Grandfather bent down. "It's a bird. A little golden bird."

Katrusya stared at the half-frozen creature cradled in her grandfather's mittens. The little bird peeped pitifully.

"How did it get here?" Katrusya asked.

"This happens when winter comes early," Grandfather explained. "Flocks of birds get caught in the snow and freeze. It is heartbreaking to see."

"Can't we do anything?" Katrusya asked.

"We can take the bird home and put it by the stove. But what good is saving one little bird when hundreds may be dying?"

"Let's look for them. Please, Grandfather! We must save the birds — as many as we can find!"

Katrusya tiptoed among the trees. *Peep! Peep! Peep!* She heard tiny voices chirping beneath the drifts. She brushed the snow aside. Underneath lay dozens of birds. Most were still alive, but so terribly frozen they could hardly open their beaks. Katrusya plucked birds from the snow, one after another.

Katrusya filled her coat. Her pockets bulged with birds. She tucked some inside each mitten and three into her scarf. Grandfather carried his share of birds, too. And still there were more.

"We'll take them home and come back for the rest," Grandfather said.

Katrusya and Grandfather arrived just as Mama was preparing breakfast. A big bowl of steaming kasha stood on the table. Katrusya opened her coat. A flock of tiny birds flew around the room.

"What is this?" cried Mama. "Where did these birds come from?"

"Oh, *Mamaniu*, we need help!" said Katrusya. "The birds are dying in the snow. Grandfather and I brought home as many as we could find, but there are still more out there."

"I'll help," said Katrusya's older sister, Lyuba, buttoning her coat.

"So will we!" said her brothers, Ivan and Danilo, setting aside their steaming bowls of buckwheat porridge. "We'll get the other boys to come, too."

"There will be more birds than can fit in one house. I'd better open the barn," said Tato, her father.

Katrusya and Grandfather returned to the forest. They did not go alone. News about the little birds spread through the village. Everyone came to help. They tucked birds inside their coats, hats, and mittens. They lined baskets with warm quilts and filled them with birds. They carried birds back to the village until all the houses and barns were full. And still there were more!

"Where can we put them?" Katrusya cried. Father Roman, the priest, came running from the village. "What is this I hear about a miracle of birds?" he asked.

"The birds need our help, Father!" Katrusya said. "There are so many! We don't have room for them all. If they're left in the snow, they will die."

"I know a place with lots of room," said Father Roman. "What better shelter for God's creatures than God's own house? Bring them to the church. There is no better deed than showing kindness to others."

Everyone carried birds to the church until there were no more to be found. The tiny creatures fluttered among the eaves like flecks of living gold. They filled the church with their chirping.

Father Roman stretched out his arms. "Welcome, little birds! Thank you for blessing us with your joyous song."

The snow stopped falling that evening, but the bitter weather continued for weeks. More snow fell. Columns of ice hung from the eaves of the houses. Trees in the forest cracked under the weight of the ice and snow. They sounded like gunshots. It was the coldest winter in memory. Not even Granny Gurko could remember one like it.

Yet, strange to say, the winter did not seem as long or as dreary as it might have. The golden birds, perched in the eaves of every home, brought a bright note of spring. In church on Sunday they chirped and trilled as the choir sang hymns. They perched on Father Roman's shoulders as he preached the sermon.

"Listen to the birds," Father Roman told the congregation. "They worship God with every chirp, with every flutter of their wings. Would that human beings had such beautiful and perfect faith!"

One morning the birds behaved strangely. They gathered by the windows, flapping their wings, chirping wildly as they flung themselves against the glass panes.

Katrusya and Grandfather hurried to ask Father Roman's advice. They were not alone. Someone from every house was there. Each person had the same question. "What is wrong with the birds?"

"They want us to let them go," Father Roman explained.

"But winter is not over yet," Katrusya protested. She did not want her friends to leave.

"Trust the birds. They know what is best," the priest told her gently.

"When must we release them?" Grandfather asked.

"On Sunday, after church."

That Sunday, Father Roman read the story of Creation, how God created the world in six days. While the birds chirped and flew about the windows, he spoke of a time to come when lions would lie down with lambs and all creatures would live in peace. Katrusya listened to every word. She hoped that time would come soon, and that Grandmother and Grandfather — even old Granny Gurko — would live to see it.

Father Roman finished by saying, "Now we must show our love for our fellow creatures. It is time to set the birds free." He walked to the doors and threw them open wide. The birds flew outside in a fluttering golden stream. "*Idit z Bogom, malenki druzi!* Go with God, little friends!" Father Roman said.

The birds circled the church and perched in the snow-covered trees, calling to the others in the houses.

"Go home. Free the birds," said Father Roman.

Katrusya and her family hurried home. Together they counted to three. Then all at once, they threw open every door and window. Every house in the village did the same. A golden flock of yellow birds filled the sky. They circled over the snow-topped roofs, then flew away toward the forest, above the trees. Within minutes they were gone.

Katrusya found herself crying. She felt as if a piece of her heart had flown away. The tears froze on her cheeks.

"God will protect the birds," Grandfather murmured. "We will see them again. I can feel it in my bones."

The rest of the winter passed slowly, like a great icicle melting drop by drop. Muddy patches appeared from beneath the snow. The sun emerged from behind the clouds. Crocuses pushed their heads above the melting ice. Spring had come at last.

And then it was Easter. Katrusya and Lyuba combed and braided each other's hair and tied it with bright ribbons. They put on new linen blouses, white as lilies, which they had woven, sewn, and embroidered themselves all through the long winter. Ivan and Danilo polished their boots until they gleamed like mirrors. Tato and Grandfather wore their finest shirts, beautifully embroidered with intricate patterns. Grandmother wore her gold earrings. Mother put on her necklace of coral beads.

As Katrusya stepped outside the house, she noticed something in the newly sprouted grass. "An egg!" she exclaimed. "An Easter egg!"

No one had ever seen an egg as beautiful as this. It was blue and gold, decorated with designs of birds flying over sheaves of wheat.

"Here's another!" cried Ivan.

"I found one, too," Danilo echoed.

The children of the village hunted everywhere. They found more beautiful eggs, dozens of them, each decorated with a unique pattern. They gathered the eggs in baskets and brought them to the church.

"Where did these eggs come from?" they asked the priest.

Father Roman laughed. "Look up!"

They all raised their eyes. The trees in the forest, the church dome, and the thatched roofs of the village were filled with birds, the same golden birds they had sheltered throughout the long winter.

"The birds have given us an Easter gift," Father Roman explained. "No two eggs are alike. Each one is different. Each one is beautiful and precious in its own way. So is every living creature in the eyes of God."

Ever since that day, in memory of the birds' gift, people have made *pysanky*, the most beautiful Easter eggs of all. They are the symbol of hope and life, of spring's triumph over winter, and of God's endless love for all creatures, great and small.

If you want to learn,
then go and ask
the wild animals and the birds,
the flowers and the fish.
Any of them can tell you
what the Lord has done.
Every living creature
is in the hands of God.

—Job 12:7-10

from The Creation

All things bright and beautiful,
All creatures great and small,
All things wise and wonderful,
The Lord God made them all.

Each little flower that opens,
Each little bird that sings,
He made their glowing colours,
He made their tiny wings. . . .

The cold wind in the winter,
The pleasant summer sun,
The ripe fruits in the garden,
He made them every one. . . .

He gave us eyes to see them,
And lips that we might tell,
How great is God Almighty,
Who has made all things well.

— *Cecil Frances Alexander*

May

A bunch of May we have brought you,
And at your door it stands,
It's but a sprout, but it's well budded out
By the work of our Lord's hands.

The moon shines bright, the stars give a light,
A little before it is day.
God bless you all, both great and small,
And send you a joyful May.

— *adapted from* "Song of the May-ers"

The second Sunday in May is Mother's Day, a time for doing something special to thank your mother for her love and care. But there are many ways in which children can show how much their mothers mean to them. Every day should be Mother's Day for you.

Jim

There never was a nicer boy
Than Mrs. Jackson's Jim.
The sun should drop its greatest gold
On him.

Because, when Mother-dear was sick,
He brought her cocoa in.
And brought her broth, and brought her bread.
And brought her medicine.
And, tipping, tidied up her room.
And would not let her see
He missed his game of baseball
Terribly.

— *Gwendolyn Brooks*

Jesus liked to teach his followers by telling stories called parables. One day, Jesus told this parable, which teaches us to listen to God so that we can grow strong in our faith.

From the Bible

A Story About a Farmer

based on MATTHEW 13:1-23; MARK 4:1-20; LUKE 8:4-15

A farmer went out to scatter seeds in a field. On his way, some seeds fell out onto the road. As he walked along, other seeds fell on rocky ground where there was not much soil. The farmer passed by some thornbushes, and some of the seeds spilled out into the thick of the bushes. Finally, the farmer got to his field, which had soil good for growing. He scattered the rest of his seeds there.

As time went on, the seeds that had fallen onto the road were stepped on or eaten by birds. The ones on the rocky ground started to grow, but they didn't get enough water and soon dried up. The seeds that spilled into the thornbushes didn't grow much, either. The bushes were so thick and prickly that there was no room for new plants to grow.

But in the field with good soil, plants grew from the seeds and made more seeds. They produced a hundred times as many seeds as the farmer had planted.

This is what the story means.

The farmer is really planting a message about God's kingdom. The seeds that fall along the road are the people who hear the message. But the devil comes along and takes it away from them, so they will not believe and be saved.

The seeds that fall on rocky ground are the people who hear the message and accept it right away. But they don't have deep roots, so they believe only for a little while. As soon as life gets hard, they give up.

The seeds that fall among the thornbushes are also people who hear the message. But they start worrying about the things they need in life and how to get rich. So there is no room for the message to get through.

The seeds that fall on good ground are the people who listen to the message and keep it in good and honest hearts. They last and produce enough plants for a good harvest.

Thanks to God

based on Psalm 65

Our God, you deserve praise. . . .

You take care of the earth and send rain to help the soil
grow all kinds of crops.
Your rivers never run dry, and you prepare the earth
to produce much grain.
You water all of its fields
and level the lumpy ground.

You send showers of rain to soften the soil
and help the plants sprout.
Wherever your footsteps touch the earth,
a rich harvest is gathered.
Desert pastures blossom,
and mountains celebrate.
Meadows are filled
with sheep and goats;
valleys overflow with grain
and echo with joyful songs.

A long time ago, in the 1800s, the United States was still being settled. Most of the people lived east of the Mississippi River. But every year, pioneer families were moving west. Pioneers who were heading for Ohio and beyond might have come across an unusual man who loved apple trees. His name was John Chapman. Born in Massachusetts, Johnny, as he was called, learned how to grow and care for apple trees while working on an orchard in Pennsylvania. Later he traveled to Ohio. He believed that God had special work for him to do.

Johnny Appleseed and the Pioneers

by Eva Moore

adapted by the author from her book *Johnny Appleseed*

Johnny Chapman had a dream of planting apple trees. He had planted one apple orchard near the town of Marietta, Ohio. Now he wanted to go farther west and bring apple trees to the pioneers in other parts of Ohio.

One day, he picked up some sacks of apple seeds and his Bible. He wore his cooking pot on his head because his hands were full. Away he walked into the wilderness.

Johnny stayed in the woods for many months, planting apple seeds here and there. When the pioneers came to clear the land for homes, they found orchards of little trees already growing. And Johnny was there, taking care of the trees, ready to sell them or give them to the pioneers.

Johnny looked very strange to the pioneers, with his ragged clothes and bare feet and his pot on his head. But they soon found that he was kind and good.

"What if Johnny is different?" they said. "He is always ready to help."

Johnny helped the men build their log cabins. He helped the women wash clothes and make candles. When people were sick, he did what he could to make them well.

The pioneers liked Johnny. They liked him so much they gave him a nickname, Johnny Appleseed.

Soon everyone had a story about this strange man who seemed to be part of the woods himself.

One pioneer said he saw Johnny playing with bear cubs in the woods, and the mother bear just stood by and watched.

Another pioneer said that when a rattlesnake bit Johnny, Johnny did not want anyone to kill it.

"The snake didn't mean it," Johnny Appleseed said. "He didn't know what he was doing."

There was another story of how someone had once given Johnny a pair of shoes to wear. It was winter and the snow was deep on the ground. Johnny didn't usually wear shoes, but he put them on and walked away. The next day, the man who gave him the shoes saw him again — barefoot.

"Where are your shoes?" the man asked.

Johnny told him he had left the shoes with a poor family he met that day. "It looked like they needed a good pair of shoes," he said.

As Johnny walked in the wilderness, there were eyes watching him from behind trees. The Indians who lived there saw Johnny planting seeds in the earth. They saw deer eat from his hand. They saw birds perch on his shoulder. They saw that he did not carry a gun.

The Indians hated the pioneers. They took the Indians' land and spoiled their hunting grounds.

The pioneers hated the Indians. The Indians sometimes attacked pioneer families. There were many battles. Men, women, and children on both sides were killed.

But the Indians would never harm Johnny Appleseed.

One day, some Indians stopped Johnny on his way along a path in the woods. Johnny followed them to their village. There the Indians gave Johnny presents of beads and fur skins. They put a feather headdress on his head, and they called him brother.

Johnny tried to keep peace between his Indian brothers and the pioneers. He was able to stop many battles just by talking to the Indians and then talking to the pioneers.

But one day, Johnny heard that an Indian tribe was going to attack a small fort in Mansfield, Ohio. There was no time to talk now. And the fort was too small to protect itself from a big attack.

Johnny didn't want to see the pioneers and Indians fighting. He had a plan.

When it was dark, Johnny ran through the wilderness. He knew the Indians would not stop him. He ran thirty miles in five hours. He ran to the fort in Mount Vernon, Ohio, where there were many soldiers. He told them about the attack the Indians were planning on Mansfield. He asked them to come with him to protect the fort.

By dawn, the soldiers were in Mansfield. The Indians who were going to attack saw them, and they went back to their village. There was no battle.

Johnny Appleseed had saved the town. He had saved the Indians, too.

God blesses those people
who are merciful.
They will be treated
with mercy!
God blesses those people
whose hearts are pure.
They will see him!
God blesses those people
who make peace.
They will be called
his children!

— Matthew 5:7–9

Dear Father, hear and bless
The beasts and singing birds,
And guard with tenderness
Small things that have no words.

— *Anonymous*

Sarah and the Kitten

adapted from the story "Soffrona and Her Cat Muff"

by Mary Martha Sherwood

Once there lived two sisters named Sarah and Sophia. Sarah was about your age, and Sophia was one year older. Every day they did their lessons together and played together like the best of friends. What a happy sight that was, for as King David says in the Bible, "It is truly wonderful when relatives live together in peace" (Psalm 133:1).

The sisters lived with their mamma in a lovely old house in the middle of pretty woods.

Sarah and Sophia loved to go out into the woods. They were always finding treasures. They found snail shells and painting stones and wild strawberries and walnuts and hazelnuts. They found beautiful moss and many kinds of flowers. They heard the songs of cuckoos and linnets and thrushes, and they saw butterflies with gold and purple plumes and dragonflies, whose wings look like fine silk netting.

One morning in the month of May, Sarah and Sophia went to play in the woods after school. They took a basket to bring home any treasures they found. It was such a pretty day, the girls walked farther than usual. They turned around a bend in the path and came to a brook. Two boys were standing by the side of the brook. They were arguing.

"Let me do it!" one boy said, grabbing at something the other was holding in his hand.

"No, I want to!" the other boy said. He bent down to the brook.

Sarah and Sophia heard a tiny mewing sound.

The boy had a little kitten in his hand. As the girls watched in horror, the boy dropped the kitten into the cold water.

"Stop!" Sophia cried out. And Sarah cried out, "You wicked boys!"

As the Bible says, "Wicked people run away when no one chases them" (Proverbs 28:1), so the boys took off as fast as they could go through the bushes.

Sarah and Sophia ran to the brook and pulled the little kitten out of the water. Sarah sat down and laid it on her lap while Sophia wiped it dry. She rubbed it and rubbed it until it was warm again. Finally, the kitten opened its eyes and began to mew.

"Oh, you dear little kitty," Sarah said. "I'm so glad you're alive! I'm going to keep you as my own pet and will call you Muff." Then she looked at her sister. "Is that all right, Sophia? Will you give me your share of her?"

Sophia could not say no. It was all the same to her, and she liked to give Sarah what she wanted. After all, she was a year older, and it was expected that she would think less of herself. Sophia had lived twelve months longer than Sarah, and how much may a person learn, with the blessing of God, in twelve months!

So it was agreed that the kitten should belong to Sarah and be called Muff. The girls put Muff into the basket upon a bed of soft moss and carried her home.

There, the girls' mamma gave them some milk to feed the little kitten. Its fur was now completely dry, and they could see that she was very beautifully marked. Her legs, face, and breast were pure white, and her back was streaked with orange and black, the coloring called calico. But she was so tiny that she was not able to lap up the milk.

Sarah and Sophia tried to feed her milk with a spoon, but the milk just ran down the outside of her little mouth and not down her throat.

Sarah was so worried about Muff that she kept the kitten in her lap while she was reading and while she was eating her supper.

The last thing Sarah did that night was to try to put some milk down Muff's throat, and this was the first thing she did in the morning. She could not think of anything else.

Indeed, she had completely forgotten that today she and Sophia had a special errand to run for their mother. They were going to see Mrs. Winters, an old woman who lived at the other side of the woods, and bring her a new shawl that they had made for her. Mrs. Winters was very poor and could not afford to buy new clothes.

Sophia packed the shawl along with some medicine the old woman needed and some tea and sugar into a basket. "Come along, Sarah," she called. "Or do you want to say at home alone today?"

Sarah came out carrying a basket of her own. "Here I am!" she called. "I couldn't leave poor little Muff behind. She's in the basket, wrapped up in a piece of warm flannel."

It was a long walk to Mrs. Winters's house. First the girls went through some dark woods where the trees met over their heads like the arches in a church. Then they crossed over a stream on a wooden bridge. Then they had to climb a steep hill covered with bushes. At last they came to a field of high grass, and in the corner of the field was Mrs. Winters's cottage.

"I hope that Mrs. Winters has some milk in her house," Sarah said, "for poor Muff must be very hungry."

The girls walked across the field and came to the cottage. The door was open and they peeked in. The cottage was very neat. Old Mrs. Winters was sitting in a rocking chair near the fireplace, needle and thread in her hand. In front of her sat a fine calico cat, the woman's only companion.

"Oh," cried Sarah from the doorway, "there's a cat! I see a cat!"

Mrs. Winters looked up from her sewing. "Hello, girls," she said. "Come in, come in."

The girls sat down on a bench. Sarah held her basket on her lap as Sophia went over to the old woman to give her the basket of gifts.

"How kind your mother is," Mrs. Winters said. "God has put goodness in her heart."

As the woman was speaking, her cat came up next to Sarah, sniffed all around the basket, and began to meow loudly. At the same time, the kitten inside the basket mewed and mewed.

"Puss, puss, pretty puss," Sarah said. She wanted to pet the cat but was a little afraid because it was quite large.

Mrs. Winters saw what was happening. "Don't worry," she said. "Tibby won't hurt you. Poor thing! She is feeling very bad just now."

"Why is that?" Sarah asked.

"Some terrible boys came in yesterday and stole her kitten," Mrs. Winters said. "I was out of the cottage picking up some sticks of wood for my fire when they sneaked in and ran off with the kitten. Since then, Tibby has been moaning and grieving like a human being."

"Oh," said Sarah, "and I do believe . . ."

"And I'm sure," said Sophia.

"And I'm so glad!" said Sarah.

"And how happy she will be!" said Sophia.

And Sarah immediately set her basket on the floor and opened it. What happiness when the mother cat saw her kitten! Mrs. Winters picked up the kitten and laid it on a mat in the corner near the fireplace. Tibby ran to the mat and lay down to give her kitten some milk. She licked it all over and talked to it in her way (that is, in the way that cats use with their kittens). Then she purred so loudly the sound filled the little cottage. It was a pleasant sight, for it is a pleasure to see anything happy.

When it was time to go, Sarah gave the kitten a little kiss. "Little puss," she said, "I am so happy for you, even though it is hard for me to leave you. But I will not be selfish. Mamma says that I can never make myself happy by making others miserable. Good-bye, little puss. If God will help me, I'll try never to be selfish." And she walked out of the cottage wiping away her tears.

Sophia turned to Mrs. Winters. "Won't you let her have Muff later, when her mother has brought her up and can part with her?"

Mrs. Winters smiled. "Of course I will, for she is a good child and said that she could never make herself happy by making others miserable."

When Muff was four months old, she was brought to Sarah, and became her cat, and lived with her until some of her orange-and-black fur had turned gray.

June

Children, you belong to the Lord, and you do
the right thing when you obey your parents . . .
Parents, don't be hard on your children. Raise
them properly. Teach them and instruct them
about the Lord.

— *Ephesians 6:1,4*

From the Bible

Abraham, Father of a Nation

based on GENESIS 12, 13, 15, 21, 25

Abraham and his family lived in the city of Haran. Their home was a tent, which they moved from place to place to tend their sheep and cattle.

One day, God came to Abraham and said, "Leave your country, your family, and your relatives and go to the land I will show you." God promised to make Abraham's name great. "Everyone on earth will be blessed because of you," He told him.

So Abraham left his homeland. He took his wife, Sarah, and his nephew, Lot, and all the people in their household. For many months they traveled from place to place with all their belongings.

Finally, they came to a rich land. But there were not enough fields for all the people and for their animals. So Abraham said to Lot, "Let's separate. If you go north, I'll go south; if you go south, I'll go north."

Lot chose to go to the lands in the east near a big city. Abraham went to the land of Canaan. Here God said to him, "Look to the north, south, east, and west. I will give you and your family all the land you can see." The Lord told him to look at the sky and try to count the stars. He said that Abraham would have as many children as there are stars in the sky.

Abraham had a son named Isaac. Isaac had two sons named Jacob and Esau. Their children had children, and their children had children, and their children had children, and their children had children. The people of Abraham numbered as many as the stars in the sky.

The Lord's Prayer

Our Father in heaven, help us to honor
your name.
Come and set up
your kingdom
so that everyone on earth
will obey you,
as you are obeyed
in heaven.
Give us our food for today.
Forgive us for doing wrong,
as we forgive others.
Keep us from being tempted
and protect us from evil.

— *Matthew 6:9-13*

Prayer for My Father

Dear Father in Heaven,
Protect my father on earth.
Watch over him at work and play
And keep him strong for us, I pray.
Stay by his side and lift him up
When troubles come to fill his cup.
Help him know
I love him so,
Dear Father in Heaven.

Our country's flag is called the Stars and Stripes. It became our official flag on June 14, 1777. Now we celebrate our flag every year on June 14, Flag Day.

Our Flag

I love to see the starry flag
That floats above my head.
I love to see its waving folds
With stripes of white and red.
"Be brave," say the red stripes.
"Be pure," say the white.
"Be true," say the bright stars,
"And stand for what's right."

— *Unknown*

Father's Day is the third Sunday in June. This legend is about a father who was put to the test and the brave son who believed in him.

The Story of William Tell

by Edward Carlton

based on *The Legend of William Tell* by Frederick Schiller

Once upon a time there was a city called Altdorf in the country of Switzerland. It was a nice enough city, but the mayor, Herr Gessler, was cruel and vain. He thought he was so special that everyone should bow down to him whenever he passed by. Anyone who didn't was in big trouble.

One day the people came out to the square in the middle of the city to find a tall pole had been put up overnight. A soft felt hat with a feather was hanging at the top of the pole.

"What could this be?" the people asked one another.

"Look!" a woman said. "Here is a sign." They all went over to read the sign at the bottom of the pole:

Notice to the people of Altdorf
By order of Herr Gessler

All who pass by this hat of your mayor
Herr Gessler

must bow to it the same as you would for
Herr Gessler himself.

Anyone who does not bow will be put in jail
for a year.

So the people went about their business. But whenever they passed the pole with Herr Gessler's hat, they did a quick bow and went on their way. It was very tiresome.

A few days later, a man and a boy came into the square in Altdorf. William Tell and his young son, Walter, who lived in the country, had not been to the city for a while and didn't know about the hat. When William Tell saw the sign, he got very angry. "Now Herr Gessler has gone too far. I bow only to God or to a worthy man, not to the likes of Gessler. And I certainly will not bow to a hat!"

The next thing he knew, some soldiers came up and grabbed his arms. They were about to drag him off to jail when who should come by but Herr Gessler himself, riding on his horse.

"What's the problem?" the cruel mayor asked the soldiers.

"This man, William Tell, will not bow to your hat, sir," one of the soldiers said. "We are taking him to jail."

"Wait," said Herr Gessler. He knew that William Tell was famous for being a very good shot with the crossbow. This gave him an idea — a cruel and vicious idea.

He turned to William Tell. "I will make a deal with you. I will pardon you and let you go free if you will do a trick with your bow and arrow. I will place an apple on your son's head and you will hit it with your arrow from one hundred paces away."

William Tell didn't know what to do. He would rather go to jail than put his son in such danger. But Walter said, "Do it, Papa. I know you won't hurt me. You are the best archer in the world."

Soon Walter was standing in the square with an apple balanced on his head. He stood tall and calm. "What a brave boy," people whispered.

William Tell counted out 100 paces and turned to face his son. He pulled an arrow from the quiver on his back and put it in his crossbow. Very slowly he lifted the bow up and took aim. He pulled the trigger and the arrow flew across the square towards the target. *Zing! Zlat!* It cut the apple right in two. Everyone cheered! William raced to his son and held him tight.

"I thank God for giving me the skill to save your life. I pray that I will never again have to live another moment like that."

Herr Gessler was the only one who was not happy. But it didn't matter. His days were numbered.

On the day he died, the people ran to the square and pulled down the pole. They set fire to the hat and cheered as they watched it burn down to a small pile of ashes, which blew away in the wind.

Once the wicked are defeated, they are gone forever,
but no one who obeys God will ever be thrown down.

— *Proverbs 12:7*

Make your parents proud, especially your mother.

— Proverbs 23:25

Just as Well

adapted from the story "So-So" by Juliana Horatia Ewing

"Be sure, my child," said the widow to her little daughter, "that you always do just as you are told."

"Very well, Mother," said the girl, whose name was Joan.

"Or at any rate, do what will do just as well," said the small dog that lay blinking near the fireplace.

"You darling!" cried the girl, and she sat down on the hearth and hugged him. But the dog got up and shook himself and moved three turns nearer the fire to get out of the way. Though her arms were soft, Joan was holding a doll in them, and the doll was made of wood, which hurts.

"What a dear, kind dog you are!" said little Joan. She was glad to have a friend who could help soften the harsh demand her mother made.

The dog was no particular kind of dog, but his fur was very smooth and he had a nice way of blinking his eyes, which made people happy to look at him. Joan and her mother had had a hard time giving him a name. They tried Faithful, Trusty, Keeper, and even Wolf, but none of these seemed to suit him. So he was called So-So, and a very nice, soft name it is.

The widow was poor, but she worked hard to keep her house in order and now and then get something special for herself and her child.

One day she was going out on business, and she called her daughter and said to her, "Now, Joan, I am going out for two hours. You are too young to protect yourself and the house, and So-So is not a very strong dog. After I go, shut the door and bolt the big wooden bar and be sure that you do not open it for any reason until I return. If strangers come, So-So will bark, which he can do just as well as a larger dog. Then they will go away."

Joan nodded. Her mother went on. "With this summer's savings I have bought a quilted skirt for you and a duffel coat for myself to keep us warm this winter. If I get the work I am going after today, I'll have enough wool to knit warm stockings for us both. So be patient until I return, and then for dinner we will have the plum cake that is cooling on the top shelf of the cupboard."

"Thank you, Mother," Joan said.

"Good-bye, my child. Be sure you do just as I have told you," said the widow.

"Very well, Mother."

Joan laid down her doll, then shut the door and fastened the big bolt. It was very heavy, and the kitchen looked gloomy when she had done it.

"I wish Mother had taken all three of us with her and had locked the house and put the key in her big pocket as she has done before," Joan said as she got into the rocking chair to put her doll to sleep.

"Yes, it would have done just as well," So-So replied as he stretched himself on the hearth.

By and by, Joan grew tired of singing lullabies to her doll. She took the three-legged stool and sat down in front of the clock to watch the hands. After a while, she sighed a big sigh.

"There are sixty seconds in every single minute, So-So," she said.

"So I have heard," said So-So. Now he was sniffing around places that he was usually not allowed to go.

"And sixty whole minutes in every hour, So-So," the girl said.

"You don't say!" growled So-So. He had not found anything good to eat. There wasn't as much as a crumb on the floor. He went to the door and sniffed under it.

"The air smells fresh," he said.

"It's a beautiful day, I know," said little Joan. "I wish Mother had allowed us to sit on the doorstep. We could have taken care of the house . . ."

"Just as well." So-So finished her sentence.

Joan stood on tiptoe to smell the air at the keyhole. As So-So had said, it smelled very fresh.

"It's not exactly what Mother told us to do," she said, "but I do believe . . ."

"It would do just as well," said So-So.

So Joan unfastened the bar and opened the door. She and the doll and So-So went out and sat on the doorstep.

The sun shone delightfully. It was an evening sun, not too hot. All day it had been ripening the corn in the field close by, and the corn glowed and waved in the breeze.

"This is just as good, and better," said Joan. "If a stranger comes, we can see him from the field path."

"Just so," said So-So, blinking in the sunshine.

Suddenly, Joan jumped up.

"Oh!" she cried, "there's a big bird. I can't see him because of the sun, but what a loud sound he makes." *Crake! Crake! Crake!* "Oh, I can see him now! He's not flying; he's running into the corn. I wish I were there. I could catch him and put him in a cage."

"I'll catch him," said So-So, and he put up his tail and started off.

"No, no!" cried Joan. "You have to stay here and take care of the house and bark if anyone comes."

"You could scream, and that would do just as well," So-So replied, with his tail still up.

"No, it wouldn't," said Joan.

"Yes, it would," So-So replied.

While they were arguing, an old woman came up to the door. She had black hair and was wearing a very old red cape.

"Good evening, my little dear," she said. "Is your family at home this fine evening?"

"Only three of us," said Joan. "I, my doll, and So-So. Mother has gone to town on business, and we are taking care of the house, but So-So wants to go after the bird we saw run into the corn."

"Was it a pretty bird?" asked the old woman.

"It was a very curious one," said Joan, "and I'd really like to go after it myself, but we can't leave the house."

"Is there no neighbor who could sit on the doorstep and keep the house while you slip down to the field?" said the old woman.

"I'm afraid not," Joan told her. "Our neighbor is sick and cannot get out of bed. Of course, if she had been able to watch the house instead of us, it would have been just as well."

"I have a long way to go this evening," the old woman said. "I wouldn't mind taking a few minutes' rest. I'll sit here on the doorstep so you can run down to the cornfield and get the bird before it flies away."

"But can you bark if anyone comes?" Joan asked her. "If you can't, then So-So must stay with you."

"I can call you and the dog if I see anyone coming, and that will do just as well," said the woman.

"So it will," little Joan replied. Off she ran to the cornfield with So-So bounding and barking ahead of her.

They did not catch the bird, though they stayed longer than they had thought they would.

"It's late," Joan said. "Mother is probably home by now. I hope she won't mind that we didn't stay in the house."

They went back up the path. Joan's mother had not come home yet. But the old woman had gone, and she had taken the quilted skirt and the duffel coat and the plum cake from the top shelf with her. And they were never seen again.

"In the future, my child," said the widow, "I hope you will always do just as you are told, whatever So-So may say."

"I will, Mother," said little Joan. (And she did.) But the dog sat and blinked. He did not dare to speak again.

I am not sure what happened to So-So. Wild dogs often change their ways and become good and faithful dogs. Sometimes they fail to become good, but when anyone begins by being only So-So, he is very apt to be So-So to the end. So-So's so seldom change.

But this So-So was *very* soft and nice, and he got no cake that dinnertime. On the whole, we will hope that he lived to be a good dog ever after.

The Wind and the Sun

from *Aesop's Fables*

The wind and the sun were having an argument.

"I'm stronger than you!" said the wind.

"No, I'm the stronger one!" said the sun.

Just then a man came walking along the road.

The sun said, "I see a way to decide who is right. Whichever one of us can make that man take off his coat will be the stronger. You begin."

So the sun went behind a cloud, and the wind began to blow on the man as hard as it could. But the harder it blew the more closely the man wrapped his coat around him. At last, the wind had to give up.

Then the sun came out from behind the cloud and shone in all its glory upon the man. The man walked on for a while. Then he found he was too hot. He took off his coat.

Kindness gets better results than force.

Out in the Fields

The little cares that fretted me,
I lost them yesterday
Among the fields above the sea,
Among the winds that play,
Among the lowing of the herds,
The rustling of the trees,
Among the singing of the birds,
The humming of the bees.

The foolish fears of what might pass
I cast them all away
Among the clover-scented grass,
Among the new-mown hay,
Among the hushing of the corn,
Where drowsy poppies nod,
Where ill thoughts die and good are born —
Out in the fields of God.

— Anonymous

July

The Lord blesses each nation
that worships only him.

— *Psalm 33:12*

Then Moses called Joshua up in front of the crowd and said: Joshua, be brave and strong as you lead these people into their land. The Lord made a promise long ago to Israel's ancestors that this land would someday belong to Israel. That time has now come, and you must divide up the land among the people. The Lord will lead you into the land. He will always be with you and help you, so don't ever be afraid of your enemies.

— Deuteronomy 31:7-8

From the Bible

Into the Promised Land

based on JOSHUA 1-6

The time of Moses came to an end. The sons and daughters of the people he had led out of Egypt had grown up. Joshua became their leader.

God told Joshua to lead the people into the land He was giving them. He said to not be afraid. He would be there to help Joshua wherever he went.

The Israelites were camped along the Jordan River. Across the river was the city of Jericho. Joshua sent two men to see what was going on in the city.

The king of Jericho found out about the spies. But a woman named Rahab hid the men on the flat roof of her house, and the king's men did not catch them.

Rahab told the spies that the people of Jericho were greatly afraid of the Israelites and their powerful God. When Joshua heard this news, he got ready to enter the city.

Rahab told the spies that the people of Jericho were greatly afraid of the Israelites and their powerful God. When Joshua heard this news, he got ready to enter the city.

God told him what to do.

Joshua led his people to the banks of the Jordan River. The first ones to reach the river were priests who were carrying the box that held the Ten Commandments. The water had come up all the way to the top of the riverbanks. How would they get the box across?

Joshua knew that God would help them. As soon as the feet of the priests touched the water, the river stopped flowing. It turned in another direction so that the riverbed dried up in front of them. The priests stood in the dry riverbed while everyone else crossed over to Jericho.

The city was shut up tight. No one went out and no one came in.

Joshua sent his army to march around the walls of the city. In the middle of the army were seven priests. They were carrying trumpets.

For six days in a row the army slowly marched once around the walls of Jericho.

On the seventh day the army marched around the walls seven times while the priests blew their trumpets. Then the priests played one loud blast on their trumpets, and all the soldiers shouted as loudly as they could. At that moment the walls around the city broke apart and came tumbling down.

The army charged into Jericho and took the city.

But they did not harm the woman Rahab and her family. This was her reward for helping the spies. She lived among the Israelites from then on.

The Israelites had come to the end of their long journey. They had come at last to the promised land.

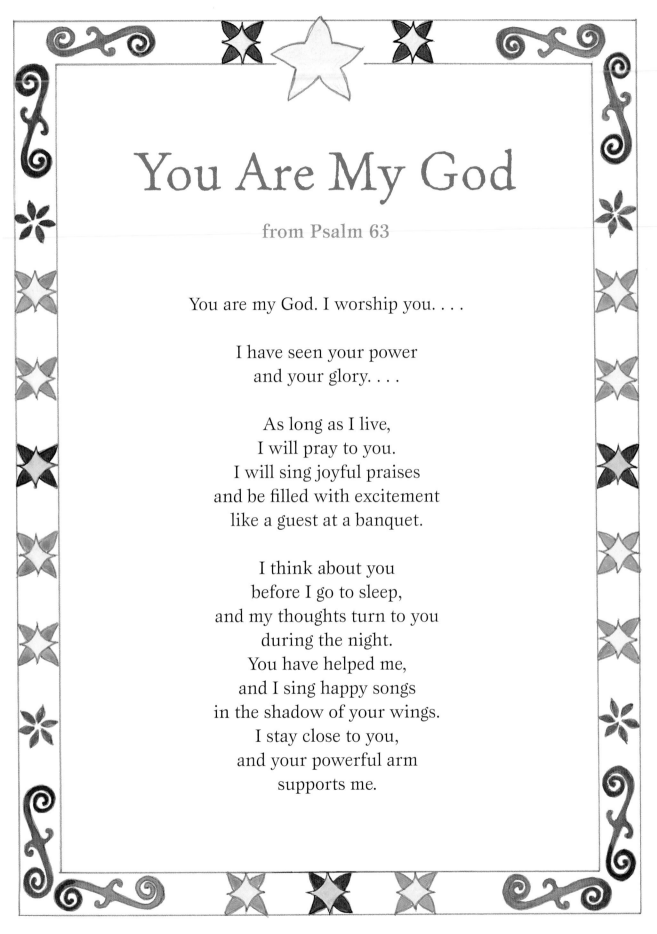

You Are My God

from Psalm 63

You are my God. I worship you. . . .

I have seen your power
and your glory. . . .

As long as I live,
I will pray to you.
I will sing joyful praises
and be filled with excitement
like a guest at a banquet.

I think about you
before I go to sleep,
and my thoughts turn to you
during the night.
You have helped me,
and I sing happy songs
in the shadow of your wings.
I stay close to you,
and your powerful arm
supports me.

July Fourth is a very important day for Americans. It marks the birth of our country more than 230 years ago.

In early 1776, the thirteen American colonies were ruled by the king of England. But on July Fourth the colonies broke away and declared themselves free and independent states, the United States of America. The king sent thousands of soldiers to win the country back.

The new country did not have much money to buy uniforms and guns for its ragtag army made up of farmers and other ordinary citizens. The English had many more soldiers, and they were much better equipped. But the United States had a special weapon — a smart and brave leader named George Washington.

Washington was put in charge of the whole army. At first, General Washington could only run away when the English attacked. Then, in the winter of 1776, everything changed.

The Old Fox

from *The Adventures of George Washington*

by Margaret Davidson

The English soldiers began to make fun of George Washington. They began to call him the Old Fox. They pretended they were hunters chasing an old fox. And the old fox always ran away.

The English chased Washington's army across the colony of New Jersey. They chased the Americans across the Delaware River into Pennsylvania. And there, on the banks of the river, the Americans stopped running. They were too tired to run any more.

They were cold and hungry. They grumbled to each other. "I don't mind staying if we get a chance to fight. But we don't fight. We've lost this war. It's no use anymore. Why not just leave?"

And many of them did leave. When night came, a man would slip out of the camp. Then another. Each morning General Washington woke to see his army smaller and smaller.

On December 18, 1776, Washington sat in his tent and wrote these words: "I think the game is pretty well up." But then he put down his pen. He wouldn't write, "We can't win." He wouldn't quit.

Washington decided to try one more time.

The American army was camped on the west side of the Delaware River. Across the river lay the town of Trenton, New Jersey. Trenton was held by fifteen hundred Hessians — German soldiers who were paid to fight for the English. Washington knew that he could not beat the Hessians if the Hessians knew he was coming. But what if he tricked them? What would happen then?

The Old Fox had a plan.

He waited until Christmas night of 1776. It was a stormy night. The snow was piling up on the ground. General Washington and his men crept out of camp. They made their way down to the river and climbed into some boats.

The river was full of ice. But Washington got his army across the water to the other side.

It was very late now. Washington could hear music coming from the town of Trenton. It was Christmas, and a few of the Hessian soldiers were still singing songs. They had eaten a big dinner and drunk a lot of wine, and now most of them were fast asleep.

Washington attacked. The Hessian soldiers didn't expect a battle that night. They jumped up and tumbled out of their tents. Bullets flew through the streets of Trenton. The Hessians were sleepy, surprised, and full of wine. Soon they gave up — still dressed in their nightshirts. The town of Trenton belonged to the Americans.

General Washington had won an important battle. But the war wasn't over yet. The English were angry when they heard about Trenton. A big English army came marching, marching across New Jersey to take Trenton back.

On January 2, 1777, the English general Cornwallis led his five thousand soldiers up to the town. And there was Washington's little army, trapped in Trenton.

It was late in the evening. "We've got him now!" General Cornwallis crowed. And he sent his men to bed. "We'll bag the Old Fox in the morning. He can't get away now."

But Washington had one more trick to play. During the night, the English campfires burned high. The American fires burned higher still. When the English saw these big fires, they thought that the Americans were trying to keep warm.

It was another trick.

During the night, the whole American army crept away into the woods. They left the great fires burning behind them.

It was snowing again, and some of the men had no shoes. Their bare feet left drops of blood in the snow. But they kept on until they left the town of Trenton far behind. It was daylight when the American army reached the town of Princeton, New Jersey, ten miles away from Trenton.

Most of the English soldiers were back at Trenton. But some English were in Princeton. Washington turned to his men. They had taken Trenton. Why not take Princeton, too? The battle of Princeton began.

Back in Trenton, General Cornwallis was just getting out of bed when he heard something that sounded like thunder. But the sky was clear. He called to one of his men, "Is that thunder I hear?"

The man listened. He looked toward the American camp. Empty! "That's not thunder," he yelled. "That's Washington's guns on Princeton!"

General Cornwallis turned his army around and raced toward Princeton. But he was too late. The Americans won there, too. And as he chased the last Englishman out of Princeton, George Washington called out, "You wanted to chase a fox. But who is the fox now?"

The war ended in 1781 when General Cornwallis surrendered to General George Washington.

George Washington became the country's first president in January 1789.

"I commend my friends, and, with them, the interests and happiness of our dear country, to the keeping and protection of Almighty God."

—George Washington in his last speech as general and commander in chief of the United States Army, December 1783

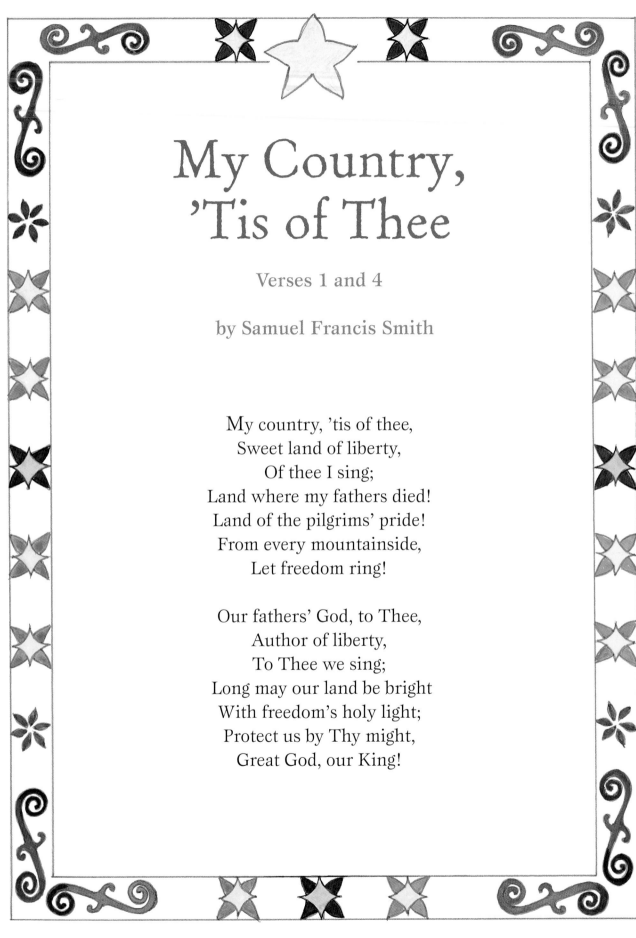

My Country, 'Tis of Thee

Verses 1 and 4

by Samuel Francis Smith

My country, 'tis of thee,
Sweet land of liberty,
Of thee I sing;
Land where my fathers died!
Land of the pilgrims' pride!
From every mountainside,
Let freedom ring!

Our fathers' God, to Thee,
Author of liberty,
To Thee we sing;
Long may our land be bright
With freedom's holy light;
Protect us by Thy might,
Great God, our King!

Knoxville, Tennessee

I always like summer
best
you can eat fresh corn
from daddy's garden
and okra
and greens
and cabbage
and lots of
barbecue
and buttermilk
and homemade ice-cream
at the church picnic
and listen to
gospel music
outside
at the church
homecoming
and go to the mountains with
your grandmother
and go barefooted
and be warm
all the time
not only when you go to bed
and sleep

— *Nikki Giovanni*

August

Look at the rising sun: there God does live,
And gives His light, and gives His heat away,
And flowers and trees and beasts and men
  receive
Comfort in morning, joy in the noonday.

from "The Little Black Boy" by William Blake

You are a kind and merciful God, and you are very patient. You always show love, and you don't like to punish anyone, not even foreigners.

— Jonah 4:2

From the Bible

Jonah and the Big Fish

based on JONAH 1-4

Jonah was a prophet who lived in the land of Israel. One day, God told Jonah to go to the distant city of Nineveh, the capital of a powerful foreign kingdom. The people there were doing evil things. Jonah was to tell them that God was so angry, He was going to punish them all.

Jonah did not want to go to Nineveh. Those people were enemies of Israel. He wanted nothing to do with them.

Instead, Jonah went to the seaport of Joppa. He bought a ticket on a ship that was going far, far away, to Spain. He was the only Hebrew on the ship.

During the trip, a storm came up. The wind blew and waves came crashing over the ship. The sailors were afraid it would sink.

"This is all your fault," one sailor said to Jonah. "Didn't you tell us that you're running away from your God? Your God must have sent the storm to punish you."

Jonah had a feeling this was so. "Throw me into the sea," he said to the sailors. "Then the storm will end."

The sailors didn't want to do it, but the storm was getting worse and worse. They threw Jonah into the sea.

At once, the storm was over and the sea became calm as glass.

Jonah sank down, down into the swirling water. Seaweed wrapped around his head. He knew he was drowning. He remembered God and prayed to Him.

Jonah did not drown in the sea. God sent a big fish to swallow him.

Jonah was safe inside the fish. He prayed to God. He thanked Him for His mercy. He promised to praise Him and honor Him.

For three days and three nights, Jonah was inside the fish. Then God commanded the fish to open its mouth and spit Jonah out.

Again, God asked Jonah to go to Nineveh. This time, Jonah went. He preached to the people about God. They turned from their wicked ways and followed God's laws. God did not punish anyone, not even foreigners.

We Thank Thee

For flowers that bloom about our feet;
For tender grass so fresh and sweet;
For song of bird and hum of bee;
For all things fair we hear or see —
　　Father in Heaven, we thank Thee!

For blue of stream, and blue of sky;
For pleasant shade of branches high;
For fragrant air and cooling breeze;
For beauty of the blooming trees —
　　Father in Heaven, we thank Thee!

For mother-love, for father-care;
For brothers strong and sisters fair;
For love at home and school each day;
For guidance lest we go astray —
　　Father in Heaven, we thank Thee!

For Thy dear, everlasting arms,
That bear us o'er all ills and harms;
For blessed words of long ago,
That help us now Thy will to know —
　　Father in Heaven, we thank Thee!

— *Ralph Waldo Emerson*

I am the Lord your God.
I am holding your hand,
so don't be afraid.
I am here to help you.

— Isaiah 41:13

Betsy and the Creepy House

adapted from chapter 1 of *Back to School With Betsy*

by Carolyn Haywood

It was a warm evening in August. Betsy was sitting on the top of the wall that ran back of the garden. Mother's garden was lovely. There were roses and spotted lilies, asters, and zinnias. The flower beds had neat borders of tiny fuzzy purple flowers.

Betsy looked down on the other side of the wall. A long time ago there had been a garden there; long, long before Betsy had learned to climb up and sit on the wall. Now there was just a wild mass of weeds and brambles and tall grass. Betsy never climbed over the wall. She didn't like anything on the other side. She didn't like the stone house that stood in the midst of the weeds and the tall grass. No one had lived in the house as long as Betsy could remember.

Sometimes Betsy would walk around the block and look up at the front of the house. It had a big porch that was covered with vines and cobwebs. Some of the windows had been broken and the chimney had fallen down. Betsy thought it was the spookiest house she had ever seen. She never told anyone, but when it was dark she was afraid to pass the house.

As Betsy sat on the wall, she looked across the weeds and tall grass. She could see the back of the house. She didn't know which looked worse, the back of the house or the front.

Just then Betsy's mother came out. "Why, Betsy," she said. "What are you looking so serious about?"

"I was just thinking," replied Betsy. "Do you suppose that anyone will ever live in that old house, Mother?"

"I wish someone *would* come to live in it," Betsy's mother said. "The For Sale sign has been hanging on it as long as we've lived here."

"Maybe if someone lived in it there would be a nice garden," said Betsy.

"Wouldn't that be lovely?" her mother replied. "Then there would be flowers on both sides of the wall."

"Well, I wouldn't want to live in it," said Betsy. "It's too dark and spooky."

Betsy got down off the wall and began to help her mother pull up some weeds.

"When does school begin, Mother?" asked Betsy.

"In a few weeks," her mother told her.

"I wonder if Miss Grey will be my teacher," Betsy said. "I love Miss Grey."

"Oh, Betsy," said her mother. "I met Miss Grey on the street the other day. She told me that she's going to be married. She isn't going to teach anymore."

Betsy straightened up and looked at her mother. "Miss Grey isn't going to be at school at all? I won't see her anymore?" she asked.

Betsy's mother looked up from the flower bed. When she saw Betsy's troubled face, she said, "Why, Betsy, darling! Of course you will see Miss Grey. I'll invite her to come and visit."

"But that won't be like school. In school, I would see her every day."

That night when Betsy went to bed, she felt very unhappy.

The next morning Betsy's friend Ellen came to play at Betsy's house. Betsy told Ellen all about Miss Grey.

Ellen felt sorry, too, when she heard that Miss Grey wouldn't be at school.

"I wish we could go to the wedding," said Ellen.

"I don't want to go to any old wedding," said Betsy. "I think Miss Grey is just a meanie to get married."

"I guess you never saw a wedding cake," said Ellen, "or you would want to go. You get a piece of cake to take home."

Just then Billy Porter arrived. Billy was in the same room in school as Betsy and Ellen.

"Hi!" shouted Billy. "What's going on?"

"Plenty," said Betsy. "Miss Grey isn't coming back to school. She's getting married and we'll never see her again."

"Married!" shouted Billy. "What does she want to get married for? She must be crazy!"

"Ellen wants to go to the wedding," said Betsy.

Billy looked at Ellen. "You must be crazy, too," he said.

"I guess you've never been to a wedding," Ellen said. "You never got any wedding cake to take home."

"What did you say?" asked Billy.

"I said, I guess you never got any wedding cake to take home," replied Ellen.

The three friends sat thinking. After a while, Betsy said, "Maybe we ought to give Miss Grey a wedding present."

"Well," said Billy, "maybe so."

"I think it would be nice," said Ellen.

"But I don't have any money," Billy said.

Neither of the girls had any money, either.

"We'll have to earn some," Billy said. "Then we'll see how much money we have for a present. I can deliver orders for Mr. Watson, the grocer."

"I can look after Mrs. Plummer's twins," said Ellen.

"Well," said Betsy, "I'll have to think up a way to make some money, too."

When Billy and Ellen left, Betsy went into the garden. She climbed up on the garden wall. She sat wondering how she could earn money for Miss Grey's wedding present.

Soon she saw a tall man coming through the weeds and the grass on the other side of the wall. Betsy was so surprised she nearly fell off the wall. She had never seen anyone there before.

The man smiled and said, "Hello. I'm Mr. Jackson. What's your name?"

"My name is Betsy," replied Betsy.

"Well, Betsy, I'm glad to meet you because you are going to be my neighbor. I've just bought this house," said Mr. Jackson, waving his hand toward the old house.

"You have?" said Betsy, in great surprise. "And will there be a garden on the other side of the wall?"

"Yes, indeed," said Mr. Jackson, "someday. But right now I have to fix up the house. It's a sight."

"It certainly is," Betsy said.

"And now," said Mr. Jackson, "I'll tell you why I came over to speak with you. There will be workmen in the house, and I would like to find someone to go over there every day after the workmen have gone to check that the doors have been locked. Do you know anyone around here who would do that for me? I'll pay a dollar a day."

Betsy looked up at the old house that gave her the creeps. *A dollar a day,* she thought. How she would love to make a dollar a day! But would she have the courage to go up to the doors of the old house?

Mr. Jackson stood waiting for Betsy to answer.

After thinking a few moments longer, Betsy said, "Do you think I could do it?"

"Why, of course you could do it!" Mr. Jackson said.

"All right," said Betsy. "I'll do it. When do you want me to begin?"

"Tomorrow," said Mr. Jackson. "The workmen leave at five o'clock.

You try the doors about quarter past five. And thank you very much indeed. I'll be back next week to pay you."

"You're welcome," said Betsy as Mr. Jackson walked away.

Betsy scrambled down off the wall and rushed home to tell her mother.

"Well, that is good news," her mother said.

"And maybe I'll earn enough money to buy Miss Grey's wedding present," said Betsy.

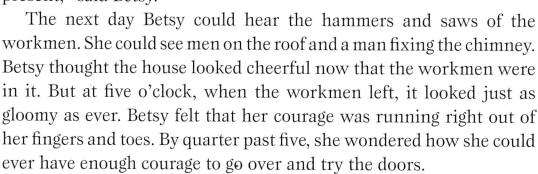

The next day Betsy could hear the hammers and saws of the workmen. She could see men on the roof and a man fixing the chimney. Betsy thought the house looked cheerful now that the workmen were in it. But at five o'clock, when the workmen left, it looked just as gloomy as ever. Betsy felt that her courage was running right out of her fingers and toes. By quarter past five, she wondered how she could ever have enough courage to go over and try the doors.

The thought came to her to ask her mother to do it. *But that wouldn't be earning the dollar,* thought Betsy. *And I don't want Mother to think that I'm a fraidy-cat.*

Betsy climbed up the wall and scrambled down the other side. The tall grass came up to her waist. Brambles scratched her bare legs. Soon she reached the old stone path that led to the back of the house. Suddenly, a little snake wriggled its way across the path. Betsy jumped. She didn't like snakes.

Betsy ran the rest of the way to the house. She ran up the steps that led to the back door. She tried the knob. The door was locked. Then she ran around to the front of the house. She went up the old, broken-down steps to the porch. She noticed that the vines had been cut away and the cobwebs were gone. She took hold of the doorknob. The front door was locked, too.

Betsy noticed that the windows on each side of the door were clean and new. She peeked through. She could see into the hall. The carpenters had begun to build new stairs. The hall was full of clean new boards. Betsy went to another window. It, too, had new glass. She looked inside. She guessed this was the living room. New bricks were piled beside the fireplace. Just then the rays of the setting sun came through the back window. They filled the room with a golden light.

Why, it isn't a creepy house at all, thought Betsy. *It's a nice house.*

Betsy walked across the porch and down the steps. As she turned the corner of the house, she saw her mother looking over the garden wall. She waved her hand to Betsy. Betsy waved back. She forgot all about the little snake as she ran along the stone path and through the tangled weeds and grass.

"Mother!" shouted Betsy. "It isn't a creepy house at all! There wasn't anything to be afraid of!"

Her mother laughed as she helped Betsy down off the wall. "Is it going to be nice?" she asked.

"It's going to be lovely," Betsy said.

That night, after her mother heard Betsy say her prayers, Betsy said, "Mother, were you standing at the garden wall all the time?"

"Yes, Betsy," replied her mother, "all the time."

"And were you watching me all the time?" asked Betsy.

"Yes, dear," said her mother, "all the time."

Betsy thought for a moment. Then she said, "That's just the way God watches me, isn't it?"

Her mother leaned over and kissed her daughter. "Yes, my precious, that is just the way God watches you."

September

Honey is good for you, my children,
    and it tastes sweet.
Wisdom is like honey
    for your life —
if you find it,
    your future is bright.

— *Proverbs 24:13-14*

From the Bible

Jesus the Teacher

based on MATTHEW 5-7

Jesus went all over Galilee, teaching the good news about God's kingdom. People came from near and far to hear him.

Jesus sat on the side of the mountain and the people sat below him. He taught them:

God blesses those people who depend only on him.
They belong to the kingdom of heaven!

God blesses those people who grieve.
They will find comfort!

God blesses those people who are humble.
The earth will belong to them!

God blesses those people who want to obey him more than to eat or drink.
They will be given what they want!

God blesses those people who are merciful.
They will be treated with mercy!

God blesses those people whose hearts are pure.
They will see him!

God blesses those people who make peace.
They will be called his children!

God blesses those people who are treated badly for doing right.
They belong to the kingdom of heaven!

Then Jesus taught the people some things they should do in order to please God.

He told them to treat others as they wanted to be treated themselves. He said that this is what the Law and the Prophets are all about. He said:

"Love your enemies, . . . and pray for anyone who mistreats you. Then you will be acting like your Father in heaven. He makes the sun rise on both good and bad people. And he sends rain for the ones who do right and for the ones who do wrong. . . .

"When you do good deeds, don't try to show off. . . .

"When you give to the poor, don't blow a loud horn. . . .

"Then your gift will be given in secret. Your Father knows what is done in secret, and he will reward you. . . .

"Watch out for false prophets! They dress up like sheep, but inside they are wolves who have come to attack you. You can tell what they are by what they do."

Jesus had many other things to teach the people. When he was finished speaking, the crowds were surprised at his teaching. He spoke so strongly that they believed his words more than the other teachers they had heard.

A Lesson for Martha

based on LUKE 10:38-41

Jesus was going to the city of Jerusalem with his twelve disciples. On the way they stopped in the village of Bethany. A friend named Martha invited them to stay for dinner.

She went to get the meal ready. In the meantime, her sister, Mary, sat down in front of Jesus. He began to tell her about God and the Kingdom of Heaven. She listened to every word.

Martha was running around preparing the dinner. There were a lot of people to feed. Finally, she went to Jesus and said, "Lord, doesn't it bother you that my sister has left me to do all the work by myself? Tell her to come and help me!"

Jesus answered, "Martha, Martha! You are worried and upset about so many things, but only one thing really matters. Mary has chosen what is best, and it will not be taken away from her."

I once walked by the field and the vineyard
of a lazy fool.
Thorns and weeds
were everywhere,
and the stone wall
had fallen down.
When I saw this,
it taught me a lesson:
Sleep a little. Doze a little. Fold your hands
and twiddle your thumbs.
Suddenly poverty hits you
and everything is gone!

— *Proverbs 24:30-34*

The Sluggard

by Isaac Watts

A sluggard is a lazy person.

'Tis the voice of the sluggard; I heard him complain,
"You have waked me too soon, I must slumber again."
As the door on its hinges, so he on his bed
Turns his sides, and his shoulders, and his heavy head.

"A little more sleep, and a little more slumber;"
Thus he wastes half his days, and his hours without number.
And when he gets up, he sits folding his hands,
Or walks about sauntering, or trifling he stands.

I pass'd by his garden, and saw the wild brier,
The thorn and the thistle grow broader and higher;
The clothes that hang on him are turning to rags;
And his money still wastes till he starves or he begs.

I made him a visit, still hoping to find
That he took better care for improving his mind;
He told me his dreams, talked of eating and drinking;
But he scarce reads his Bible, and never loves thinking.

Said I then to my heart, "Here's a lesson for me,"
This man's but a picture of what I might be:
But thanks to my friends for their care in my breeding,
Who taught me betimes to love working and reading.

The Rooster, the Mouse, and the Little Red Hen

Once upon a time, there was a hill. And on the hill there was a pretty little house. It had one green door and four little windows with green shutters, and inside lived a Rooster and a Mouse and a little Red Hen.

On another hill close by there was another little house. It was very ugly. It had a door that wouldn't shut and two broken windows, and all the paint was off the shutters.

In this house there lived a big bad Fox and four little foxes.

One morning these four bad little foxes came to the big bad Fox and said, "Oh, Father, we are so hungry!"

The big bad Fox was hungry, too. He thought it was about time for him to go hunting for their next meal. Where would they find something tasty to eat? The big bad Fox looked out one of the broken windows. *Aha!* he thought.

Then he said to his bad little foxes, "On the hill over there I see a house. And in that house lives a Rooster."

"And a Mouse!" screamed two of the little foxes.

"And a little Red Hen!" screamed the other two.

"And they are nice and fat," went on the big bad Fox. "This very day, I will take my great sack, and I will go up that hill and in that door, and into my sack I will put the Rooster, and the Mouse, and the little Red Hen."

"I will make a fire to roast the Rooster," said one little fox.

"I will put on the saucepan to boil the Hen," said the second.

"And I will get the frying pan to fry the Mouse," said the third.

"And I will have the biggest helping when they are all cooked," said the fourth, who was the greediest of all.

Then the four little foxes jumped for joy, and the big bad Fox went to get his sack ready to start upon his journey.

But what was happening to the Rooster, the Mouse, and the little Red Hen all this time?

Well, sad to say, the Rooster and the Mouse got out of bed on the wrong side that morning. The Rooster said the day was too hot, and the Mouse said the day was too cold.

They came grumbling down to the kitchen, where the good little Red Hen, looking as bright as a sunbeam, was bustling about.

"Who will get some sticks to make the fire?" she asked.

"Not me," said the Rooster.

"Not me," said the Mouse.

"Then I will do it myself," said the little Red Hen.

So off she ran to get the sticks.

"Now, who will fill the kettle from the spring?" she asked.

"Not me," said the Rooster.

"Not me," said the Mouse.

"Then I will do it myself," said the little Red Hen. And off she went to fill the kettle.

"Now, who will get the breakfast ready?" she asked, as she put the kettle on to boil.

"Not me," said the Rooster.

"Not me," said the Mouse.

"Then I will do it myself," said the little Red Hen.

All during breakfast the Rooster and Mouse quarreled and grumbled.

The Rooster upset the milk jug and the Mouse scattered crumbs all over the floor.

"Who will clear away the breakfast?" asked the poor little Red Hen, hoping they would soon stop being so cross.

"Not me," said the Rooster.

"Not me," said the Mouse.

"Then I will do it myself," said the little Red Hen.

So she cleared everything away, swept up the crumbs, and brushed up the fireplace.

"Now," she said, "who will help me make the beds?"

"Not me," said the Rooster.

"Not me," said the Mouse.

"Then I will do it myself," said the little Red Hen.

And she hopped away up the stairs.

The lazy Rooster and the Mouse each sat down in comfortable armchairs by the fire and soon fell fast asleep.

Now the bad Fox had crept up the hill and into the garden, and if the Rooster and the Mouse had not been asleep, they would have seen his sharp eyes peeping in at the window.

Rat, tat, tat. Rat, tat, tat, the Fox knocked at the door.

"Who can that be?" asked the Mouse, opening his eyes halfway.

"Go look for yourself if you want to know," said the rude Rooster.

Perhaps it is the postman, and he may have a letter for me, thought the Mouse to himself. So without waiting to see who it was, he lifted the latch and opened the door.

As soon as he opened it, in walked the big Fox with a cruel smile upon his face.

"Oh! Oh! Oh!" squeaked the Mouse as he tried to run up the chimney.

"Doodle doodle do!" screamed the Rooster as he jumped on the back of the biggest armchair.

The Fox only laughed, and without more ado — *pop* — into his bag went the Mouse and — *pop* — into the bag went the Rooster. The little Red Hen came running downstairs to see what all the noise was about, and — *pop* — into the bag went the little Red Hen.

Then the Fox took a long piece of string out of his pocket and wound it around and around and around the mouth of the sack and tied it very tightly indeed. He threw the sack over his back, and off he started down the hill.

The sun was very hot, and soon Mr. Fox began to feel that his sack was heavy, and at last he thought he would lie down under a tree and go to sleep for a while. He threw the sack down with a big bump and very soon fell fast asleep.

Snore, snore, snore, went the Fox.

As soon as the little Red Hen heard this, she took out her scissors and began to snip a hole in the sack, just large enough for the Mouse to creep through.

"Quick," she whispered to the Mouse, "run as fast as you can, and bring back a stone just as large as yourself."

Out scampered the Mouse, and soon he came back dragging the stone after him.

"Push it in here," said the little Red Hen, and he pushed it into the bag in a twinkling.

Then the little Red Hen snipped away at the hole until it was large enough for the Rooster to get through.

"Quick," she said, "run just as fast as you can, and bring back a stone just as big as yourself."

Out flew the Rooster, who soon came back, quite out of breath, with a big stone, which he pushed into the sack, too.

Then the little Red Hen popped out, found a stone just as big as herself, and pushed it in.

Then she put on her thimble, took out her needle and thread, and sewed up the hole as quickly as she could.

When it was done, the Rooster and the Mouse and the little Red Hen ran home very fast, shut the doors after them, locked the bolts, shut down the shutters, drew down the blinds, and felt quite safe.

The bad Fox lay fast asleep under the tree for some time, but at last he woke up.

"Dear me," he said, rubbing his eyes. Looking at the long shadows on the grass, he said, "How late it is getting. I must hurry home."

The bad Fox went rumbling and groaning down the hill until he came to a stream. *Splash!* In went one foot. *Splash!* In went the other. But the stones in the sack were so heavy that with his very next step, down tumbled Mr. Fox into the deep water. And then the fishes carried him off to their caves and kept him there, so he was never seen again. And the four greedy little foxes had to go to bed that night without any supper.

But the Rooster and the Mouse never grumbled again. Next morning, they lit the fire and filled the kettle. They laid the breakfast and did all the work while the good little Red Hen had a holiday and sat resting in the big armchair.

No foxes ever troubled them again, and for all I know, they are still living happily in the little house with the green door and the green shutters that stands on the hill.

The Thirsty Crow

from Aesop's Fables

A crow, half dead with thirst, came upon a jar. He looked inside and saw that there was a little bit of water left at the bottom! He put his beak inside the jar to drink. But his beak was too short.

He tried and he tried and he tried, but he could not get his beak down deep enough to reach the water.

The crow was so thirsty! He thought and he thought. Maybe he could push the jar over and then drink the water as it spilled out. But no, most of the water would just run off.

Then the crow had a better idea. He saw that there were small bits of rocks all around him. He put his head down, picked up one of the pebbles in his beak, and dropped it into the jar.

Then he took another pebble and dropped it into the jar. Then he took another pebble and dropped that into the jar. Then he took another pebble and dropped that into the jar. Then he took another pebble and dropped that into the jar. Then he took another pebble and dropped that into the jar.

At last, at last, he saw the water rise up higher in the jar. After putting in a few more pebbles, he was able to drink the water and save his life.

Use your head, not just your muscle.

October

When the wind blows
The leaves fall free
Yellow leaves falling
In golden air.

And everywhere
Upon the ground
Leaves of gold
Are scattered round.

— *Margaret Wise Brown*

Children, you show love for others by truly helping them, and not merely by talking about it.

— 1 John 3:18

From the Bible

The Real Neighbor

based on LUKE 10:25-37

In his teachings, Jesus often said, "Love your neighbors as much as you love yourself."

One day, he was teaching in the Temple in the city of Jerusalem and someone asked him, "Who are my neighbors?"

Jesus answered him by telling him this story.

❧

A man was traveling along a road from Jerusalem to Jericho. Some robbers started to follow him. They grabbed him and beat him up. They took everything he had and ran off, leaving him lying in the road.

Soon a priest from the Temple came along the same road. He saw the injured man. Did the priest run over to help him? No. He crossed the road and went on his way.

Later, a man who worked in the Temple came along. Did he rush over to help the injured traveler? No. He, too, crossed the road and went on his way.

Then another man came along the road, riding on a donkey. This man was a stranger in the area. He was a Samaritan from the land called Samaria. Did the Samaritan cross the road and go on his way, too?

No. He stopped immediately when he saw the injured man. He got off his donkey and went to see if he could help. He put bandages on the man's wounds. Then he lifted the man onto the donkey and took him to the nearest inn.

The Samaritan stayed with the injured man all night and looked after him.

The next morning, the good Samaritan gave the innkeeper two silver coins and said, "Please take care of the man. If you spend more than this on him, I will pay you when I return."

When he finished the story, Jesus asked, "Which one of these three people was a real neighbor to the man who was beaten up by robbers?"

The listener said, "The one who showed pity."

Jesus said, "Go and do the same!"

✒

Today, two thousand years after Jesus told this story, the words "good Samaritan" mean a person who goes out of his way to help someone in need.

Pleasing the Lord

— MATTHEW 25:31-40

When the Son of Man comes in his glory with all of his angels, he will sit on this royal throne. The people of all nations will be brought before him, and he will separate them, as shepherds separate their sheep and goats.

He will place the sheep on his right and the goats on his left. Then the king will say to those on his right, "My father has blessed you! Come and receive the kingdom that was prepared for you before the world was created. When I was hungry, you gave me something to eat, and when I was thirsty, you gave me something to drink. When I was a stranger, you welcomed me, and when I was naked, you gave me clothes to wear. When I was sick, you took care of me, and when I was in jail, you visited me."

Then the ones who pleased the Lord will ask, "When did we give you something to eat or drink? When did we welcome you as a stranger or give you clothes to wear or visit you while you were sick or in jail?"

The king will answer, "Whenever you did it for any of my people, no matter how unimportant they seemed, you did it for me."

Kindness is rewarded — but if you are cruel,
you hurt yourself.

— *Proverbs 11:17*

The Fox and the Mask

from *Aesop's Fables*

A fox somehow got into the storeroom of a theater. He was poking around when suddenly he saw a face staring at him! He jumped in fright.

But then he looked closer. He found it was only a mask, such as an actor wears over his face.

"Ah," said the fox to the mask, "you look very fine. It's a shame you don't have any brains."

Outside show is a poor substitute for inner worth.

The Jay and the Peacocks

from *Aesop's Fables*

A plain, gray-colored jay happened to go into a yard where peacocks came to walk every day. He found a number of feathers that had fallen from the peacocks when they were molting.

The jay picked up all the feathers and tied them to his tail. He strutted across the yard in front of some peacocks.

When he came near them, the peacocks could see he was a phony. They ran up to him and pulled off all his borrowed feathers.

There was nothing the jay could do but go back to the other jays, who had been watching all this time. They were just as annoyed with him as the peacocks and told him,

"It is not only fine feathers that make fine birds."

Trust the Lord! Be brave and strong and trust the Lord.

— Psalm 27:14

Saint George and the Dragon

retold by Jan White

Saint George is the patron saint of England and one of the most famous of Christian figures. He lived more than 1,500 years ago and was declared a saint around the year 900.

George was such a beloved saint that people began to tell stories of his bravery and goodness. The story of Saint George and the dragon was first written down in the year 1265. Different versions of the tale have been told ever since then. The story has been around for so long that no one knows how much of it is really true. But we know that people still like to tell it because it honors one of the great heroes of the Christian church.

A long time ago, there was a land that was lush with palm trees and fragrant with spices. In that land was a walled city, and beside the city was a deep, clear lake. Oh, how the children of the city laughed as they raced to play at the water's edge! Their mothers walked more slowly, balancing water jars on their heads while herding their flocks of sheep.

One day, as the children came running down to the lake, they noticed that the water, usually so clear, had grown murky. Suddenly, the lake began to boil, and it almost disappeared under a cloud of steam. Then a great and terrible dragon rose out of the churning waters. The dragon stomped and snorted. It opened its enormous mouth, and flames of fire shot out. As the children and their mothers ran screaming to hide behind the city's high stone walls, the dragon spied the sheep on the hill near the lake. In one gulp, it ate them all.

"What are we going to do about this dragon?" the people asked the king. "It will destroy the whole city!"

The king fingered his fine, rich robe. He had never faced this kind of danger before, but he was sure he could take care of one single dragon.

"We will slay the dragon!" the king declared.

And so one of the king's soldiers was dressed in armor and given a big, sharp sword. The people cheered as the man marched out of the city gates and toward the lake.

But the brave swordsman never came back. Nor did the next one, or the one after that. The rest of the soldiers refused to go.

The king called a meeting of his council. He told them, "If we cannot slay the beast, we must think of another way to stop it from killing us all."

The members of the council sat in silence. Finally, one of them said, "If the dragon gets enough to eat, maybe it won't attack us. We have plenty of sheep. Let's give it two sheep a day."

"So be it!" the king said.

And so they sacrificed two sheep to the dragon every day. This seemed to work. For a time, the beast was satisfied and left them alone. But soon there were few sheep left. The people realized that their herds would not last much longer.

The king grew grave. He climbed the city's walls. From their height, he could see the dragon, its tail lashing the foul swamp that had once been a crystalline lake. How could he save the city?

The king called another meeting of the council. In this desperate situation, the members knew they had to do something drastic. In the end, they came up with a solution that filled them all with sorrow. Instead of giving the dragon two sheep every day, they would give the monster one sheep and one human being. The names of all the young people in the city would be put into a basket. Every family had to participate. Each day one name would be drawn at random.

"So be it," the king said with a heavy heart.

Days passed. Each morning a name was drawn, and each day another child perished to save the rest. One child, two children, three. At night, the walls of the city echoed with the sounds of their mothers wailing in sorrow.

One morning, as fate would have it, the name of the king's daughter was drawn. The king put his arms around his only daughter. He offered to give the people whatever riches they wanted if they would spare her. But the people would not listen. Had he not agreed to sacrifice the children? Had he himself not said that every family must offer its young? It didn't matter that the king wore a crown of gold or owned piles of riches. He was no better off than they.

The king clasped his daughter's hands. "I had hoped to dance at your wedding," he said, his eyes full of tears. "I had hoped to see you bear children, and to set my crown upon their heads." He buried his face in her hands. "Oh," he cried, "I wish that I had not lived to see this day!"

The princess knelt down at her father's feet to receive his blessing. Then, slowly, she made her way out of the gates of the city and stumbled toward the lake. The tearful king and all the townspeople stood at the walls watching.

But before the princess reached the lake, a rider came galloping along the road to the city. He was dressed in a suit of silver armor and carried a shield decorated with a red cross. The rider stopped when he saw the young girl all in tears. He got off his horse to ask her what was the matter.

The stranger was George of Cappadocia, a land far away. He had served in the Roman army, where he had earned the rank of tribune. As tribune it had been his duty to care for and protect the common people, not the powerful. Now he continued to do good deeds in the name of Jesus Christ. He went to the aid of anyone who was in need of help.

The princess shook her head sorrowfully. "Good youth," she said, "get back on your horse and go while you are able! I am to die, and there is no help for it. But you should not die, too."

George glanced up and saw the king and the others watching from the wall.

"Tell me what ails you," he insisted. "I will not take one step away until you do."

And so the princess told him the whole story. As she was talking, the dragon reared its head out of the lake.

The princess cried out, "Go, brave knight! Save yourself!"

The dragon pulled its huge body out of the water and came toward George on dreadful feet with claws like sharpened knives. George felt the heat of the dragon's fiery breath upon his face. He stumbled backward, but then he summoned all his courage. He prayed to God for help.

Quickly, George got back on his horse and drew his sword. He rode up to the dragon, holding his shield high. At the sight of the red cross, the dragon froze in fear. Then George pulled his sword and dealt the evil monster a terrible blow that sent it reeling to the ground.

"Don't be afraid," he said to the princess. "Take the sash from your waist and tie it around the dragon's neck. It will not hurt you now."

When the princess did this, the dragon rose meekly to his feet, following the princess back to the gates of the city as tamely as a week-old lamb.

When the people saw the dragon coming toward the city, they fled, taking cover in the caves that nestled in the surrounding hills. George called them back.

"You have nothing to fear," he told them. "The Lord has brought me here so that I might save you from the monster. If you believe in Christ, be baptized in his name and I will slay the beast."

The people looked at George. His faith shone before them as brightly as the sun itself. That day, twenty thousand men and many thousands of women and children were baptized. Then George raised his sword and cut off the head of the dragon. A great hurrah arose.

Because George had saved the princess, and the city as well, the king offered him a great sum of money. George accepted the reward, but he did not keep a coin for himself. He gathered the poor of the city — those who were hungry, those who were ill and ill cared for — and gave all the money to them.

"Do not forget," George said to the king, "to always care for the church of God, honor the priests, and look after the poor."

With that, George mounted his horse. The people watched as he rode off. Then they loaded the dragon onto a cart, hitched it with four yoke of oxen, and hauled the hulking, lifeless body to be buried far, far away.

from
Life Doesn't Frighten Me

Shadows on the wall
Noises down the hall
Life doesn't frighten me at all.

Bad dogs barking loud
Big ghosts in a cloud
Life doesn't frighten me at all.

Mean old Mother Goose
Lions on the loose
They don't frighten me at all.

Dragons breathing flame
On my counterpane
That doesn't frighten me at all.

I go boo
Make them shoo
I make fun
Way they run
I won't cry
So they fly
I just smile
They go wild.

Life doesn't frighten me at all.

— *Maya Angelou*

November

Tell the Lord
how thankful you are,
because he is kind
and always merciful.

— *Psalm 118:1*

The Ant and the Grasshopper

from *Aesop's Fables*

In a field one summer's day, a grasshopper was hopping about, chirping and singing to its heart's content. An ant passed by carrying an ear of corn. It was a very heavy load, but he did not stop. He was taking the corn to his nest.

"Why not come and play with me?" said the grasshopper. "The day is too nice to be working so hard."

"I am helping to lay up food for the winter," said the ant. "I think you should be doing the same."

"Why worry about winter?" the grasshopper said. "We have plenty of food now."

The ant was tired from his work, and he thought it would be fun to join the grasshopper. But he went on his way and went on working until he had filled his nest with corn.

Winter came as it always does, and the grasshopper had no more food to eat. He was dying of hunger while the ants were eating every day from the corn they had stored away. Then the grasshopper knew that

it is best to prepare for the hard days ahead.

The Story of the Two Sons

based on LUKE 15:11-32

There once was a man who had two sons. The older son stayed at home. He worked hard in the fields.

The younger son wasn't happy at home. When he was old enough, he took his share of the family's money and left home.

The young man went to another country and lived a wild life. He didn't care how much money he spent as long as he was having fun. In a few years, the money ran out. The fun stopped.

Now the young man was miserable. He didn't even have a penny to buy a bit of bread.

There was only one thing he could do. He went back home.

His father was working out in the fields. He looked up and saw his son all ragged and dirty. He ran to him and hugged and kissed him.

The son told his father he had lived a bad life and was sorry. "I am no longer good enough to be called your son," he said.

But his father was happy to have him back. He gave him sandals and new clothes. He got everything ready for a big feast to celebrate.

This made the older son angry. He had worked hard for his father. But his father had never made a big feast in his honor.

The father told him, "My son, everything I have is yours. But we should celebrate and give thanks! Your brother was dead, but now he is alive. He was lost, but now he has been found."

The Lord is my God!
I will praise him and tell him
how thankful I am.

— *Psalm 118:28*

From the Bible

Jesus Feeds Five Thousand

based on MATTHEW 14:13-21; MARK 6:30-44;
LUKE 9:10-17; JOHN 6:1-14

A great crowd of people had come to see Jesus and hear him speak. Five thousand men and many more women and children were gathered on a hill. Jesus was tired, but he could not turn them away. He saw that they were like sheep without a shepherd. He healed the sick among them and then began to teach them about God.

The people stayed all day. Jesus' disciples told him, "The people are getting hungry. Let them leave so they can go to the villages near here and buy something to eat."

Jesus answered, "They don't have to leave. You give them something to eat."

The twelve disciples looked around to see what food they had. The disciple Andrew came back with a small basket. "A boy gave me these five small loaves of bread and two fish. But what good is that with all these people?"

Jesus told the people to sit down on the grass. He held up the five loaves of bread and two fish. He looked up to Heaven and gave thanks for the food. Then he broke the bread and fish into pieces and gave them to his disciples. The disciples passed food out to the people.

There was enough for everyone! And after everyone was full, there were enough leftovers to fill twelve large baskets.

Giving Thanks at Mealtime

Bless us, O Lord,
and these Your gifts, which we are about to receive
from Your goodness, through Christ our Lord.
Amen.

First the seed and then the grain;
Thank You, God, for sun and rain.
First the flour and then the bread;
Thank You, God, that we are fed.
Thank You, God, for all your care;
help us all to share and share.
Amen.

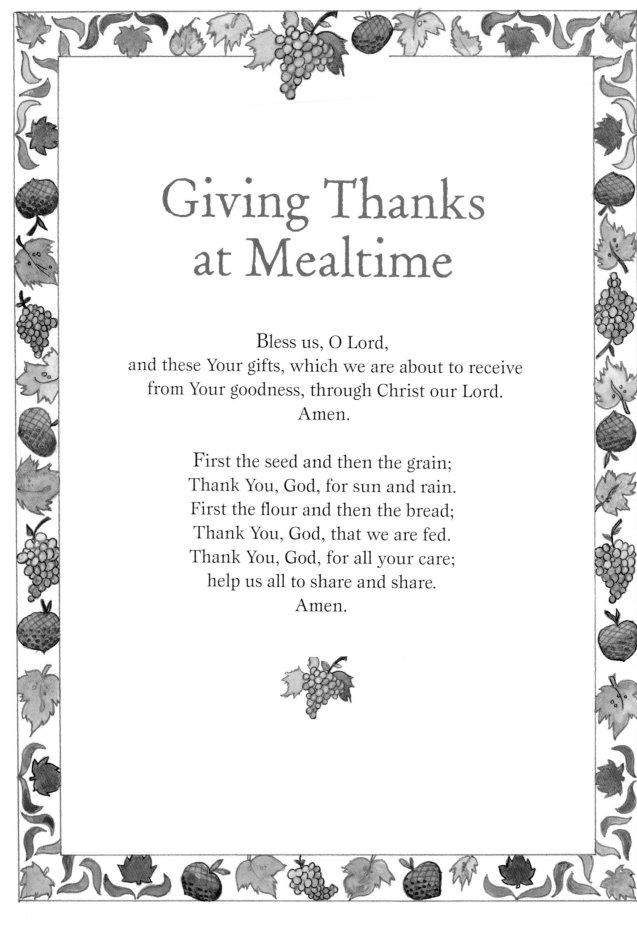

Each Thanksgiving we think about the Pilgrims. The Pilgrims were among the first people to settle in America. They sailed across the ocean from England in the year 1620 because they were not free to worship God the way they wanted to in their homeland.

When their ship, the *Mayflower*, left England, there were 102 passengers on board. Twenty-two of them were children age eighteen or younger. When the *Mayflower* got to Plymouth Rock, Massachusetts, there were 104 passengers. This story tells what happened.

New Pilgrims

from chapter 5 of Margaret Pumphrey's *Pilgrim Stories*,

revised and expanded by Elvajean Hall

On and on the ship sailed. Some days were full of sunshine and the sea was smooth. Then mothers were able to cook, building little fires in the sandboxes belowdecks. How good hot stew tasted after days of gnawing on cheese and hardtack!

The children begged to play outside after weeks belowdecks, but the crew said no. It was bad enough, they thought, having 102 people jammed in where there was space for a dozen at most. They weren't going to put up with more than twenty young ones running around and getting in the way.

Sometimes Priscilla Mullins would keep them quiet by telling stories. Even the tired mothers who were too far away to hear the words of the story would smile as they looked at Priscilla's laughing eyes.

"What a comfort that Mullins girl is," they said to each other.

Then Mary Chilton would take her turn, and John Alden, the cooper, would whittle out a puzzle or toy from some of his barrel staves. Even some of the sailors who had said they hated the children relented enough to teach the boys how to tie knots.

And so the long weeks dragged by. There was no heat on the *Mayflower*, no toilet except a bucket that had to be emptied overboard, no bathroom, no way to get cleaned up. Like their parents, the children wore the same clothes day after day, week after week, getting dirtier and shabbier all the time.

All night, every night, someone was coughing, as nearly everyone had caught cold. When tired children cried in their sleep, "I want to go home, Mama," weary mothers tried to soothe them so they would not wake all the others.

One day, when the voyage was nearly over, there was a big surprise. The Hopkinses had a baby brother. Giles wanted to name him Dick after his cat back home. But that name did not please his parents at all. Some of the children who had been born in Holland suggested Jan. But Elizabeth and Stephen Hopkins liked that even less than they liked Dick.

"This is an English baby and not a Dutch baby," they said.

Then someone suggested, "Why not give him a new name, one that nobody has ever heard before?" What could it be?

"Mayflower?" No, that sounded too much like a girl's name.

This will never do, thought Mrs. Hopkins when another week passed, and still the baby had no name. "Constance, you have never told us what you would like to call your baby brother."

"Oh, I think Ocean would be as good a name as any!"

"Ocean!" Mrs. Hopkins laughed. "What a queer-sounding name that is! I am sure no other child in the world has ever been called Ocean."

When Elder Brewster heard of the new suggestion he was pleased. "I know of a word in another language that means ocean. It would make a better-sounding name. It is Oceanus."

"Oceanus Hopkins! That is a good name!" exclaimed the baby's father. And so the first Pilgrim boy to be born on the *Mayflower* was called Oceanus.

Not many days later another baby was born on the *Mayflower*, which was by that time at anchor off Cape Cod. He also had to have a name.

"Wandering, let's call him Wandering!" suggested several of the children at once. "Wandering, because that's what we are always doing!"

Mrs. White did not like Wandering for a name, and so for the second time the oldest Pilgrim on the ship was asked for his advice. Did he know another nice-sounding word that meant the same as Wandering?

This time Mr. Brewster suggested Peregrine.

Peregrine White and Oceanus Hopkins! What big names for such tiny red babies, thought most of the children.

Children named in this story:
Priscilla Mullins, age 18
Mary Chilton, age 15
Giles Hopkins, age 12 or 13
Constance Hopkins, age 14 or 15

First Thanksgiving

Three days we had,
feasting, praying, singing.

Three days outdoors at wooden tables,
Colonists and Indians together.
Celebrating a full harvest,
A golden summer of corn.

We hunted the woods, finding
Venison, deer, and wild turkey.

We brought our plump geese and ducks,
Great catches of silver fish.

We baked cornmeal bread with nuts,
Journey cake, and steaming succotash.

We roasted the meat on spits
Before huge, leaping fires.

We stewed our tawny pumpkins
In buckets of bubbling maple sap.

Three days we had,
feasting, praying, singing.

Three days outdoors at wooden tables,
Colonists and Indians together,
Celebrating a full harvest,
Praying, each to our God.

— *Myra Cohn Livingston*

December

I have good news for you, which will make everyone happy. This very day in King David's hometown a Savior was born for you. He is Christ the Lord.

— Luke 2:10-11

My Gift

What can I give Him,
Poor as I am?
If I were a shepherd
I would bring a lamb,
If I were a Wise Man,
I would do my part, —
Yet what can I give Him,
Give my heart.

— *Christina Rossetti*

Jesus Is Born

based on LUKE 2:1-7

Mary was a young woman who lived in the village of Nazareth in a part of Israel called Galilee. Something special was going to happen to Mary very soon. She was going to have a baby.

While Mary and her husband, Joseph, were waiting for the baby to be born, they got some news. The emperor of Rome, who ruled over all the land of Israel, had made an order. Everyone in the land was to pay taxes to Rome. To do this, each family had to go to their hometown to be counted.

And so Mary and Joseph had to go to Joseph's hometown of Bethlehem. Bethlehem was in Judea, many miles south of Nazareth. It was also called the city of David, because the great King David had been born there. Joseph was from David's family.

The journey was long. After three days, Joseph and Mary came to Bethlehem. But they could not find a place to stay. At last, they came to an inn. There was no room at the inn, but the innkeeper told them they could stay in the stable. The animals would keep them warm.

Here in the stable, Mary's baby was born. She called him Jesus. She wrapped him in swaddling clothes and laid him on a bed of hay in a manger.

That night there were shepherds watching their sheep in the fields near Bethlehem.

An angel came down to them from the Lord. The brightness of the Lord's glory shined around them. The shepherds fell to their knees and put their hands over their eyes. They were very frightened.

But the angel said to them, "Don't be afraid! I have good news for you, which will make everyone happy. This very day in King David's hometown, a Savior was born for you. He is Christ the Lord. You will know who he is because you will find him lying on a bed of hay in a manger."

Suddenly, many other angels came down from Heaven. They said, "Praise God in Heaven! Peace on earth to everyone who pleases God."

The shepherds went to Bethlehem. They found Jesus lying in the manger. They told Mary and Joseph what the angels had said about their son. Mary thought about this. She wondered what it meant.

As the shepherds went back to their sheep, they could not stop talking about the baby and praising God.

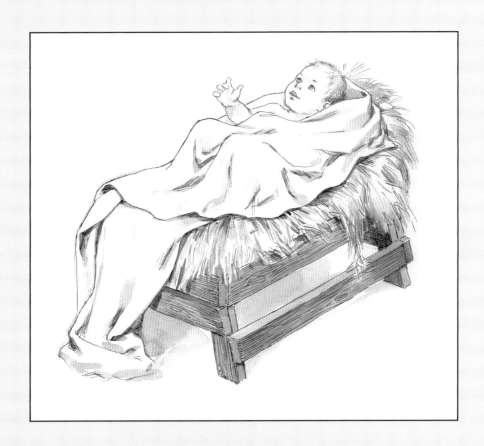

Away in a manger, no crib for a bed,
The little Lord Jesus laid down his sweet head.
The stars in the sky looked down where he lay,
The little Lord Jesus, asleep on the hay.

Special Visitors

based on MATTHEW 2:1-12

The same night that Jesus was born in Bethlehem, three Wise Men who lived far away in the East saw a bright new star in the sky. They knew the star meant that a great new king had been born. They set out to follow the star so they could worship the new leader.

The Wise Men traveled a long, long distance, always keeping the bright star in sight. At last they came to the city of Jerusalem in Judea. How much farther did they have to go to find the newborn king?

"This is the palace of King Herod, who rules this part of the country," one of the men said. "Surely he will know. Let's ask him."

The Wise Men bowed to King Herod. "Where is the child born to be king of the Jews?" one of them asked King Herod. "We saw his star in the east and have come to worship him."

King Herod didn't know anything about the baby. But he was very worried. Was this baby meant to grow up and take away his crown as ruler of Judea? He asked the Wise Men to wait and then called together the priests and teachers. "Where will this new king be born?" he asked them.

They told him, "He will be born in Bethlehem, just as the prophet wrote long ago:

'Bethlehem in the land of Judea,
you are very important among the towns of Judea.
From your town will come a leader,
who will be like a shepherd for my people Israel.'"

It is just as I feared! King Herod said to himself. But he pretended to be glad. He went back and told the Wise Men that they should go to Bethlehem. "When you find the child," he said, "let me know. I want to go and worship him, too." (Herod only said this so he could find the child and be sure he did not live long enough to rob him of his kingdom, no matter what the prophet had said.)

The star went ahead of the Wise Men until it stopped over the house where the child was. The men went into the house and found the child with his mother, Mary.

The visitors got down on their knees to worship the baby Jesus. They gave him special gifts they had brought with them—precious gold, and the sweet and strong-smelling spices of frankincense and myrrh. They all gave thanks to God for sending the baby Jesus.

Later they went back home by another road. They had been warned in a dream not to go back to Herod.

O little town of Bethlehem,
How still we see thee lie!
Above thy deep and dreamless sleep,
The silent stars go by.
Yet in thy dark streets shineth
The everlasting Light;
The hopes and fears
of all the years
Are met in thee tonight.

In the Great Walled Country

adapted from the story by Raymond Alden

Far away up at the north end of the world is a land called the Great Walled Country. It got its name because all around the country is a wall, hundreds of feet thick and hundreds of feet high. The wall is made of ice and never melts, winter or summer. For this reason not many people have ever seen the place.

The land is filled with children, for nobody who lives there ever grows up. The king and queen, the princes and princesses, and members of the court may be as old as you please, but they are children, too. They play a great deal of the time, but they make excellent rulers and everyone is pleased with the government.

There are all sorts of curious things about the way they live in the Great Walled Country, but this story is only about their Christmas.

You can just imagine what fun their Christmas must be, so near to the North Pole, with ice and snow everywhere. But that's not all. Grandfather Christmas lives just on the north side of the country, so close that his house leans against the great wall for support. (Grandfather Christmas is his name in the Great Walled Country. In other places he might be called Santa Claus.)

Having Grandfather Christmas for a neighbor has many advantages. For one, he takes care of all the Christmas gifts for the children in the Great Walled Country. On the day before Christmas, just before he sets out to deliver presents in the rest of the world, he goes into a huge forest of Christmas trees that grows behind the king's palace and fills the trees with toys and books and all sorts of good things.

When night comes, the children dress up in warm clothes and go to the forest to gather gifts for their friends. The forest is so big that there is room for everyone to wander among the trees and choose gifts for their friends in secret. No one ever thinks of taking a present for himself. This is the way they have been celebrating Christmas for hundreds of years.

But one time, many years ago, the children of the Great Walled Country had a very strange Christmas. Early that year, a visitor came to the land. He was the first stranger in a long, long time who had been able to get over the wall of ice.

The stranger told the king and queen that he was an explorer. He talked for hours about all the places he had been. Then he asked the king about the Great Walled Country. He wanted to know all about their customs and holidays.

When the king told him how they celebrated Christmas, the explorer laughed. "That is very interesting," he said, "but I should think that children who have Grandfather Christmas for a neighbor could find a better and easier way to get their presents. Why don't you each choose your own presents when you go into the forest on Christmas Eve? No one can tell what you want as well as you can."

The king thought this was a very wise idea, and so did the queen and the other members of the royal court. They all agreed that they had been very foolish never to have thought of this before.

So the king sent out an announcement to all the children of the land. The plan seemed as wise to them as it had to the king and queen. Everyone had at some time been a little disappointed with their Christmas gifts. Now there would be no danger of that.

꒱

The stranger was soon gone from the country. The seasons passed until at last it was Christmastime again.

Now, on Christmas Eve the children always got together at the palace and sang carols until it was time to go into the forest. On this particular night it seemed to the king that the music was not quite as merry, and the children's eyes did not shine as gladly as in other years. But there could be no good reason for this, since everyone was expecting a better time than usual, so he thought no more about it.

There was, however, one person at the palace that night who was not pleased with the new plan about Christmas gifts. This was a boy named Peter, who lived not far from the palace with his sister Rose. Rose's legs were crippled and she could not walk. She spent her days in a chair by the window, looking out at the world beyond their little house.

Peter took good care of his sister and tried to make her happy in every way he could. On Christmas he had always gone to the forest and returned loaded with pretty things for Rose. And although she was not able to go there and get presents for her brother, he did not mind. He always got plenty of gifts from his friends.

But now, Peter wondered, what about Rose? Under the new plan, they could only go out once and take gifts for themselves. All of Peter's friends were busy planning what they would pick, but his poor sister could not go one step toward the forest.

After thinking for a long time, Peter knew there was only one thing he could do.

That night, the children made their way in starlight that was so bright it almost showed their shadows on the sparkling snow. As soon as they came to the edge of the forest, they set out, eager to see the trees all full of wonderful things.

Ten minutes later, if you had been in the forest, you would have seen the children standing with tears running down their cheeks. For as they searched the low-bending branches, they saw nothing. Had Grandfather Christmas forgotten them, or had there been some dreadful accident that kept him away?

As the children went sadly trooping out of the forest dragging their empty bags behind them, some of them came upon Peter. His bag was so full it seemed it would burst.

"Isn't this the best Christmas ever?" he called out to his friends. "Grandfather Christmas has never been so good to us before."

"Why, what do you mean?" one of the other children said. "There aren't any presents in the forest at all."

"No presents?" said Peter. "I have a bag full of them." But he did not open the bag to show the others. He did not want them to see he had not done as the king had ordered. The presents in his bag were all for Rose and not for himself.

"I left many more than I took," Peter told the others. "Come and see." Following his own footprints, Peter led his friends back into the woods. "There they are! See them shining on the trees?"

But no one saw anything but ordinary evergreens. Peter must be walking in his sleep, the others thought. Maybe he's dreaming he found presents, but his bag is really just full of pine cones.

On Christmas Day there was sadness all through the Great Walled Country. But those who came to the house of Peter and his sister saw plenty of books and dolls and beautiful toys piled up around Rose's chair. When they asked where these things came from, Rose said, "Why, from the Christmas Tree forest, of course." But how could that be? There had been no gifts on the trees!

The only one who could solve the mystery was Grandfather Christmas himself. So the king asked three of the princes to go to see Grandfather Christmas that very day.

Getting over the wall of ice was not easy, but at last the princes reached the other side. They slid down the chimney of Grandfather Christmas's house. Inside they found the old man sound asleep.

The princes shook him gently until he woke up. He sat up, rubbing his eyes.

One of the princes spoke. "Grandfather Christmas, sir . . . we have come from the Great Walled Country. The king wants to know why you forgot us and left no presents in the forest this year."

"I never forget you," said Grandfather Christmas. "The presents were there. You did not see them, that's all."

The princes told him that the children had searched the whole forest and no one had found any presents.

"Indeed?" said Grandfather Christmas. "What about Peter? Didn't he find presents?"

Then the princes were silent, for they had heard about the gifts at Peter's house.

"You had better go home," said Grandfather Christmas, "and let me finish my nap. The presents were there, but they were never intended for children who were looking only for themselves. I am not surprised you did not see them." And he turned over and went back to sleep.

᠅

The next December, the king sent out another official announcement. This year everyone must seek out gifts for others in the Christmas Tree forest in the old way.

So that is what they have been doing ever since. And in order that they do not forget what happened (in case anyone should ever ask for another change), the king reads to them every year from their Big Book the story of the sad Christmas when they had no gifts.

I heard a bird sing
In the dark of December
A magical thing
And sweet to remember.

"We are nearer to Spring
Than we were in September,"
I heard a bird sing
In the dark of December.

— *Oliver Hereford*

Let's Carol

Let's carol in the city streets;
Let's sing across the snow;
Let's pause at every doorstep
In the candlelight's glow
Beside the wreath of holly,
Beneath the mistletoe—
To sing the ancient wonder song,
The song of long ago.

Let's tell the Christmas story
Of silent Bethlehem,
Of how the stars one midnight
Became a diadem*;

How love flamed in a halo
Around a Virgin's head,
And how a Child was crowned a king
Upon a manger bed.

Let's carol in the city streets;
Let's sing across the snow;
Let's sing the ancient wonder song,
The song of long ago!

— *Rowena Bennett*

*A diadem is a royal headband, a kind of crown

Sources

"Abe Speaks Out" by Frances Cavannah. From the book *Abe Lincoln Gets His Chance* by Frances Cavannah. Copyright © 1959 by Rand McNally & Company. Copyright © under international copyright union by Rand McNally & Company.

"Betsy and the Creepy House" by Carolyn Haywood. Adapted from *Back to School with Betsy* by Carolyn Haywood. Copyright © 1971 by Carolyn Haywood. Used by Permission of Harcourt Brace Jovanich.

"The Birds' Gift" by Eric A. Kimmel. Text copyright (c) 1999 by Eric A. Kimmel. All rights reserved. Reprinted from *The Birds' Gift: A Ukrainian Easter Story* by permission of Holiday House, Inc.

"First Thanksgiving" by Myra Cohn Livingston. Copyright © 1975 by Myra Cohn Livingston. Reprinted from *Merrily Comes Our Harvest In* by Lee Bennett Hopkins (1978 HBJ).

"God Is Like This" by Rowena Bennett. From *The Day Is Dancing and Other Poems* by Rowena Bennett. Text copyright © 1948,1968, by Rowena Bennett. Used by permission of Follett Publishing Company.

"There's Someone I Know" by Jack Prelutsky. From *It's Valentine's Day* by Jack Prelutsky. Text copyright (c) 1983 by Jack Prelutsky. Used by permission of HarperCollins Publishers.

"Jim" by Gwendolyn Brooks. From *Bronzeville Boys and Girls* by Gwendolyn Brooks. Copyright (c) 1956 by Gwendolyn Brooks. Reprinted by consent of Brooks Permissions.

"Johnny Appleseed and the Pioneers" by Eva Moore. From *Johnny Appleseed* by Eva Moore. Copyright © 1964 by Eva Moore. Published by Scholastic Inc.

"Knoxville, Tennessee" by Nikki Giovanni. Copyright (c) 1968, 1970 by Nikki Giovanni. Reprinted by permission of Nikki Giovanni.

"Let's Carol" by Rowena Bennett. From *The Day Is Dancing and Other Poems* by Rowena Bennett. Text copyright © 1948,1968, by Rowena Bennett. Used by permission of Follett Publishing Company.

"Life Doesn't Frighten Me" by Maya Angelou. Copyright (c) 1978 by Maya Angelou from *And Still I Rise* by Maya Angelou. Reprinted by permission of Random House, Inc.

"The Old Fox" by Margaret Davidson. From *The Adventures of George Washington* by Margaret Davidson. Copyright (c) 1965 by Margaret Davidson. Reprinted by permission of Scholastic Inc.

"Singing for Dr. King" by Angela Shelf Medearis. From *Singing for Dr. King* by Angela Shelf Medearis. Copyright (c) 2004 by Angela Shelf Medearis. Reprinted by permission of Scholastic Inc.